T0281153

Lecture Notes in Computer Science 3204

Commenced Publication in 1973
Founding and Former Series Editors:
Gerhard Goos, Juris Hartmanis, and Jan van Leeuwen

Carlos Andrés Peña Reyes

Coevolutionary
Fuzzy Modeling

 Springer

Author

Carlos Andrés Peña Reyes
Swiss Federal Institute of Technology
Logic Systems Laboratory LSL - IC - EPFL
CH 1015, Lausanne, Switzerland
E-mail: c.penha@ieee.org

Library of Congress Control Number: 2004113303

CR Subject Classification (1998): F.1, F.4, I.2

ISSN 0302-9743
ISBN 3-540-22994-9 Springer Berlin Heidelberg New York

Springer is a part of Springer Science+Business Media

springeronline.com

© Springer-Verlag Berlin Heidelberg 2004
Printed in Germany

Typesetting: Camera-ready by author, data conversion by Boller Mediendesign
Printed on acid-free paper   SPIN: 11312918   06/3142   5 4 3 2 1 0

with love...

to Sandra, my wife, for being there

to Paula, my daughter, for having arrived

Foreword

As we all know only too well, computers are rigid, unbending, unyielding, inflexible, and quite unwieldy. Let's face it: they've improved our lives in many a way, but they do tend to be a pain ... When interacting with them you have to be very methodical and precise, in a manner quite contrary to human nature. Step outside the computer's programmed repertoire of behavior, it will simply refuse to cooperate, or—even worse—it will "crash" (what a vivid term computing professionals have coined to describe a computer's breaking down!). Computers are notoriously bad at learning new things and at dealing with new situations. It all adds up to one thing: At their most fundamental computers lack the ability to *adapt*.

Adaptation concerns a system's ability to undergo modifications according to changing circumstances, thus ensuring its continued functionality. We often speak of an environment, and of the system's adjustment to changing environmental conditions. The archetypal examples of adaptive systems are not among Man's creations, but among Nature's: From bacteria to bumblebees, natural organisms show a striking capacity to adapt to changing circumstances, a quality which has not escaped the eyes of computing scientists and engineers. The influence of the biological sciences in computing is on the rise, slowly but surely inching its way toward the mainstream. There are many examples today of systems inspired by biology, known as *bio-inspired* systems.

Adaptation comes in many guises and forms. For one, computers are *crisp* creatures whereas we humans are *fuzzy*. So can we (beneficially) narrow this gap? There are two possible ways to go about this. The first is by forcing humans to behave more crisply—to be precise and unambiguous; this is exactly the stance that computer programmers must assume: Since they converse in the computer's tongue, they must be very "mechanic," avoiding the use of imprecise concepts. There is another way to narrow the human-computer gap, though, which is much less "painful" to us: having the computer behave in a fuzzier manner. Can this be done—can we "fuzzify" computers? Yes—by using so-called *fuzzy logic*.

Fuzzy logic made its appearance in 1965, when Lotfi Zadeh, then at the University of California, Berkeley, published a paper entitled *Fuzzy Sets*. The field has gained prominence over the past two decades, finding its way beyond academic circles into industry: Many successful commercial applications—fuzzy systems—have been built to date, ranging from washing machines to medical diagnostic systems.

Perhaps the biggest obstacle in the field is that of design: How does one go about designing a fuzzy system, with all of its multifarious, interdependent parameters? In this book, Carlos Andrés Peña-Reyes presents a highly efficient methodology to overcome this debilitating obstruction, by resorting to Nature's modus operandi for designing complex systems: Evolution.

Natural evolution is a powerful force: It has brought about a plethora of complex machines—such as eyes, wings, and brains—the construction of which are still well beyond our current engineering capabilities. If natural evolution is so successful a designer, why not simulate its workings in an engineering setting, by using a computer to evolve solutions to hard problems? Researchers pursuing this idea in the 1950s and 1960s gave birth to the domain of evolutionary computation. Four decades later, the domain is flourishing—both in industry and academia— presenting what may well be a new approach to optimization and problem-solving.

Marriage, as discovered by social designers long ago, is a powerful force, able to bring about genius, ingenious, and heterogenous (albeit sometimes arsenious) offspring. Harnessing this unifying force of nature, Dr. Peña-Reyes has produced a winning offspring by marrying evolutionary computation and fuzzy logic. And, most propitiously, the marriage certificate itself—this book you know hold—is a joy to read!

Enjoy...

April 2004   Moshe Sipper

Preface

Anything is one of a million paths. [...] I warn you. Look at every path
closely and deliberately. Try it as many times as you think necessary.
Then ask yourself, and yourself alone, one question: [...] Does this path
have a heart? [...] A path without a heart is never enjoyable. You have
to work hard even to take it. On the other hand, a path with heart is easy;
it does not make you work at liking it. **For my part** there is only the
traveling on paths that have heart, on any path that may have heart. There
I travel, and the only worthwhile challenge is to traverse its full length.
And there I travel looking, looking, breathlessly.

Don Juan Matus,
quoted by Carlos Castaneda in The Teachings of Don Juan

Human thinking and in particular our capacity to make decisions has long interested scientists: philosophers, physiologists, psychologists, mathematicians, engineers. Philosophers are interested in the motivations and the implications of decisions, physiologists and psychologists in the different mechanisms leading to them,
and mathematicians and engineers in obtaining a model that permits the reproduction of this capacity. The research presented in this book goes in this latter direction:
it proposes a methodology for modeling and reproducing human decision-making
processes.

Rather than seeing this research as the culmination of an effort, I prefer to see
it like a landmark in a path ... my path with heart. This book exists thanks to the
support and the teachings of many people. In particular, five people had direct effect
on its contents and on its form: Sandra Parra, Moshe Sipper, Andrés Pérez-Uribe,
Daniel Mange, and Eduardo Sánchez. To them, my most sincere and grateful ac-
knowledgment. Each person we cross in our life modifies a little the course that
our path can take. My gratitude goes to all those people—teachers, friends, and
family—whose presence has modeled my path.

This book introduces *Fuzzy CoCo*, a novel approach for system design, conducive to explaining human decisions. Based on fuzzy logic and coevolutionary
computation, Fuzzy CoCo is a methodology for constructing systems able to accurately predict the outcome of a decision-making process, while providing an understandable explanation of the underlying reasoning. Fuzzy logic provides a formal framework for constructing systems exhibiting both good numeric performance
(precision) and linguistic representation (interpretability). From a numeric point of

view, fuzzy systems exhibit nonlinear behavior and can handle imprecise and incomplete information. Linguistically, they represent knowledge in the form of rules, a natural way for explaining decision processes. Fuzzy modeling—meaning the construction of fuzzy systems—is an arduous task, demanding the identification of many parameters. This book analyzes the fuzzy-modeling problem and different approaches to coping with it, focusing on evolutionary fuzzy modeling—the design of fuzzy inference systems using evolutionary algorithms—which constitutes the methodological base of my approach.

The central contribution of this work is the use of an advanced evolutionary technique—cooperative coevolution—for dealing with the simultaneous design of connective and operational parameters. Cooperative coevolutionary fuzzy modeling succeeds in overcoming several limitations exhibited by other standard evolutionary approaches: stagnation, convergence to local optima, and computational costliness.

Designing interpretable systems is a prime goal of my approach, which I study thoroughly herein. Based on a set of semantic and syntactic criteria, regarding the definition of linguistic concepts and their causal connections, I propose a number of strategies for producing more interpretable fuzzy systems. These strategies are implemented in Fuzzy CoCo, resulting in a modeling methodology providing high numeric precision, while incurring as little a loss of interpretability as possible.

The application of Fuzzy CoCo is validated by modeling the decision processes involved in three problems: Fisher's iris data, a benchmark problem, and two breast-cancer diagnostic problems, the WBCD problem and the Catalonia mammography interpretation problem. Several aspects of Fuzzy CoCo are then thoroughly analyzed to provide a deeper understanding of the method. These analyses show the consistency of the results. They also help derive a stepwise guide to applying Fuzzy CoCo, and a set of qualitative relationships between some of its parameters that facilitate setting up the algorithm. Finally, this work proposes and explores preliminarily two extensions to the method: Island Fuzzy CoCo and Incremental Fuzzy CoCo, which together with the original CoCo constitute a family of coevolutionary fuzzy modeling techniques.

Morges, Switzerland   Carlos Andrés Peña-Reyes
June 2004

Table of Contents

1 Introduction

Human thinking and in particular our capacity to make decisions has long interested scientists from many disciplines: philosophy, medicine, psychology, mathematics, and engineering, among others. Philosophers are interested in the motivations and the implications of decisions, physicians and psychologists in the different mechanisms leading to them, and mathematicians and engineers in obtaining a model that permits the reproduction of this capacity. The central aim of this research is to propose a methodology to attain this latter goal: modeling and reproducing human decision making processes.

1.1 General Context

1.1.1 Problem Description

The general problem that motivates the research is the development of an approach to automatically construct systems which predict, as accurately as possible, the outcome of a human decision-making process while providing an understandable explanation of a possible reasoning leading to it. Such systems should, as much as possible, deal with the features of the information involved in human decisions: imprecise, incomplete, ambiguous, and subjective.

Human decision-making processes involve many factors, from factual information to intuitionistic relations, that are hard to explain, even for the person making the decisions (whom we call the *expert*). Acquiring, or transmitting expertise (i.e., the knowledge required to make decisions in a given domain) involves one or more of the following knowledge-processing tasks: formalization, ordered presentation, experiment-driven verification and validation, and continuous actualization based on experience. This is a long process, and a human can take up to several years to reach a satisfactory level of expertise in critical domains. Nowadays, with the increasing amount of available information and the development of new technologies, many domains require the shortening of acquiring, transmitting, and updating knowledge. Computer-based systems may provide the tools necessary to do this.

Present-day databases contain a huge amount of data concerning human decisions that should be used to model decision-making processes. These data are, however, just a collection of recorded facts that do not contain by themselves any information or knowledge useful to explain or to predict the decisions. There exist

C.A. Peña Reyes: Coevolutionary Fuzzy Modeling, LNCS 3204, pp. 1-26, 2004.
© Springer-Verlag Berlin Heidelberg 2004

many methods that, based on these data, can build systems to predict the outcome of a given decision. Albeit useful and widely used, these methods and systems lack the explanatory power required to transmit knowledge to humans.

It thus becomes necessary to produce systems that, besides proposing accurate predictions, also provide human-understandable explanations of the decisions made. Note that the goal herein is not to model the actual human reasoning process, but only to express the knowledge behind a decision in a manner conducive to human understanding. As with many other human activities, decision-making involves information that is inherently imprecise, often ambiguous, and sometimes incomplete. The systems developed should be able to deal with such information, and still provide accurate predictions and understandable explanations.

Many human tasks may benefit from, and sometimes require, decision explanation systems. Among them one can cite client attention, diagnosis, prognosis, and planning. In client attention, the person or system in charge usually requires vast knowledge to answer simple questions. Diagnostic tasks involve the interpretation of many facts to identify the condition of a system. Prediction implies the analysis of actual conditions to predict the future development of a system. Planning tasks involve deciding on actions that, once performed, would drive a system to a desired condition. There exists a domain that concerns all these tasks and several others, where decisions must be made and accompanied by explanations: medicine. Indeed, in medical practice it is customary to perform patient examination, diagnosis of risks and diseases, prognosis of a disease development, and treatment planning. Medicine is thus a domain where explanatory systems might bring many advantages.

Building explanatory systems is a difficult task. An extended approach, used to build so-called expert systems, is based on knowledge gathered directly from experts. One applies a process, known as *knowledge engineering*, which starts by collecting raw knowledge from diverse experts, continuing by systematically organizing and formalizing this knowledge, finally producing an explanatory system capable of providing sufficiently accurate predictions. Such knowledge construction is a lengthy task that involves many people from diverse domains, and long sessions of knowledge gathering, formalization, and validation with experts. Despite the fact that it is costly and time-consuming, knowledge engineering is still the best alternative to designing large and hierarchic explanatory systems (i.e., involving hundreds of input variables, and tens of chained, hierarchical decisions).

Other approaches for building explanatory systems take advantage of available data to support many design stages, extracting the knowledge embedded in the data and representing such knowledge in a manner accessible to humans. These approaches render knowledge engineering more automatic, as the role of the expert is reduced to delimiting the problem and validating the soundness and the coherence of the extracted knowledge.

1.1.2 Proposed Solution

The solution I propose, called *Fuzzy CoCo*, is a novel approach that combines two methodologies—fuzzy systems and coevolutionary algorithms—so as to automatically produce accurate and interpretable systems. The approach is based on two elements: (1) a system model capable of providing both accuracy and human understandability, and (2) an algorithm that allows to build such a model from available information.

To represent the knowledge, I chose fuzzy systems, which may attain good numeric performance and provide a scheme to represent knowledge in a way that resembles human communication and reasoning. Fuzzy systems exhibit some characteristics that render them adequate to solving the problem tackled herein:

1. They represent knowledge in the form of rules, a natural way to explain decision processes.
2. They express concepts with linguistic labels, close to human representation (e.g., "high fever" instead of "temperature higher than 39.3 degrees").
3. Such linguistic representation (i.e., concepts and rules) is accompanied by a precise numeric equivalent that is adequate for managing information available in a numeric way.
4. Fuzzy systems are adequate to model nonlinear behaviors, exhibited by almost all natural processes.
5. Fuzzy systems have proven to be universal approximators, meaning that provided enough rules and concepts, they can approximate any numeric behavior with the desired precision level (at the cost of reduced linguistic expressiveness).

The construction of fuzzy models of large and complex systems is a hard task, demanding the identification of many parameters. To better understand this problem—i.e., the fuzzy modeling problem—I propose a classification of fuzzy parameters into four classes: logic, structural, connective, and operational. This classification serves as a conceptual framework to decompose the fuzzy modeling problem, to understand how existing modeling techniques deal with this problem, and to propose novel techniques to solve it efficiently.

As a general methodology for constructing fuzzy systems I use evolutionary computation, a set of computational techniques based on the principle of natural selection. Evolutionary algorithms are widely used to search for adequate solutions in complex spaces that resist analytical solutions. Specifically, I use an advanced evolutionary technique, cooperative coevolution, which deals particularly well with requirements of complexity and modularity, while exhibiting reasonable computational cost.

The search for interpretability in evolutionary fuzzy modeling is represented by several constraints taken into account when designing the evolutionary algorithm. However, there is no well-established definition for interpretability of fuzzy systems serving to define these constraints. Based on some works that have attempted to define objective criteria to reinforce interpretability, I define two groups of criteria—semantic and syntactic—and propose some strategies to satisfy them.

The resulting approach, Fuzzy CoCo, is a fuzzy modeling technique, based on cooperative coevolution, conceived to provide high numeric precision (accuracy), while incurring as little a loss of linguistic descriptive power (interpretability) as possible. In Fuzzy CoCo, two coevolving, cooperative species are defined: rules and membership functions (which define linguistic concepts). The interpretability of the resulting systems is reinforced by applying the strategies proposed with this aim. Fuzzy CoCo proves to be very efficient in designing highly accurate and interpretable systems to solve hard problems, in particular modeling medical diagnostic decision processes.

1.1.3 Outline of the Book

The methodology proposed is based on two domains: fuzzy logic and evolutionary computation. The rest of this chapter is dedicated to presenting some basic notions of these two fields, necessary for the subsequent chapters. Section 1.2 presents fuzzy systems and Section 1.3 introduces evolutionary computation.

The fusion of these two domains gives rise to evolutionary fuzzy modeling, the subject presented in Chapter 2. This chapter starts (Section 2.1) presenting in detail the fuzzy-modeling problem, including a novel classification of fuzzy system parameters, that provides some key ideas important to the conception of Fuzzy CoCo. After presenting the application of evolutionary computation to fuzzy modeling in Section 2.2, the chapter continues with an original discussion on interpretability issues in Section 2.3. The subject is illustrated in Section 2.4 with an example application to a real-world medical problem.

Chapter 3 presents Fuzzy CoCo, a novel cooperative coevolutionary approach to fuzzy modeling. After introducing coevolutionary algorithms (Section 3.1) and cooperative coevolution (Section 3.2), Section 3.3 presents in detail the algorithm. Section 3.4 concludes the chapter by presenting a simple application of Fuzzy CoCo to a flower classification problem.

Chapter 4 presents the application of Fuzzy CoCo to modeling the decision processes involved in two breast-cancer diagnostic problems. First, the Wisconsin breast cancer diagnosis problem (Section 4.1) illustrates the capabilities of the method, comparing it with recent works. The systems found to solve the second problem, the Catalonia mammography database (Section 4.2), have led to the design of an operational online breast-cancer risk assessor.

Several aspects of Fuzzy CoCo are thoroughly analyzed in Chapter 5. These aspects are: application (Section 5.1), effect of parameters on performance (Section 5.2), consistency and quality (Section 5.3), and local generality (Section 5.4), a non-conventional measure applied to single fuzzy systems. Generality is complementary and closely related to generalization tests that are applied to modeling methods and not to the systems it produces.

Chapter 6 sketches two extensions to Fuzzy CoCo: Island Fuzzy CoCo, described in Section 6.1, and Incremental Fuzzy CoCo, delineated in Section 6.2. The goal of proposing these two extensions is to simplify the task of finding an adequate size of the rule base, a critical user-defined parameter in Fuzzy CoCo. Each extension is accompanied by preliminary tests performed to explore its behavior.

Finally, Chapter 7 presents some conclusions, summarizes the goals achieved in the present work, and recaps the original contributions made. The chapter ends with several considerations on possible future work derived from this research.

1.2 Fuzzy Systems

A fuzzy inference system—or simply a fuzzy system—is a rule-based system that uses fuzzy logic, rather than Boolean logic, to reason about data. Fuzzy logic is a computational paradigm that provides a mathematical tool for representing and manipulating information in a way that resembles human communication and reasoning processes [121]. It is based on the assumption that, in contrast to Boolean logic, a statement can be *partially* true (or false), and composed of imprecise concepts. For example, the expression "I live near Geneva," where the fuzzy value "near" applied to the fuzzy variable "distance," in addition to being imprecise, is subject to interpretation. The foundations of Fuzzy Logic were established in 1965 by Lotfi Zadeh in his seminal paper about fuzzy sets [122]. While research and applications of fuzzy sets have grown to cover a wide spectrum of disciplines [120], the present work concentrates on its use in rule-based systems.

In this section I present some concepts of fuzzy logic and fuzzy systems necessary for my work. In the next subsection I introduce basic notions of fuzzy sets and fuzzy logic. Then, in Section 1.2.2 I briefly present concepts related to propositional fuzzy logic: linguistic variables and conditional fuzzy statements. Next, I describe the steps involved in the fuzzy inference process in Section 1.2.3 to finally present, in Section 1.2.4, what a fuzzy inference system is and explain its functioning based on a simple example.

For more detailed introductions to fuzzy logic and fuzzy inference systems, the reader is referred to [57, 120, 121]

1.2.1 Basic Notions of Fuzzy Sets and Fuzzy Logic

1.2.1.1 Fuzzy Sets. Recall that an ordinary, or *crisp*, set A in a universe of discourse U can be defined by listing all its members or by defining conditions to identify the elements $x \in A$ (i.e., $A = \{x \mid x$ meets some condition$\}$). The characteristic function, generally called *membership function*, associated with A is a mapping $\mu_A : U \rightarrow \{0, 1\}$ such that for any element x of the universe, $\mu_A(x) = 1$, if x is a member of A and $\mu_A(x) = 0$, if x is not a member of A. The example in Figure 1.1 shows the membership function characterizing the crisp set $A = \{x \mid 20 \leq x \leq 26\}$).

Fuzzy sets are a generalization of crisp sets. A fuzzy set F defined on a universe of discourse U is characterized by a membership function $\mu_F(x)$ which takes values in the interval $[0, 1]$ (i.e., $\mu_A : U \rightarrow [0, 1]$). Note that the term membership function makes more sense in the context of fuzzy sets as it stresses the idea that $\mu_F(x)$ denotes the degree to which x is a member of the set F. The operation that assigns

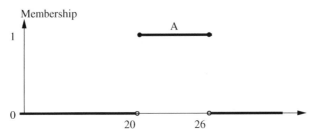

Fig. 1.1. Membership function of a crisp set. The crisp set is defined as $A = \{x \mid 20 \leq x \leq 26\}$.

a membership value $\mu(x)$ to a given value x is called *fuzzification*. The example in Figure 1.2 shows the membership function of the fuzzy set $F = \{x \mid x \text{ is between } 20 \text{ and } 26\}$ (i.e., the fuzzy set representing approximately the same concept than the crisp set of Figure 1.1), together with the fuzzification of an example value.

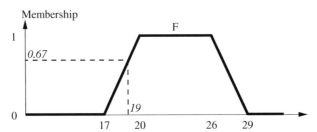

Fig. 1.2. Membership function of a fuzzy set. The fuzzy set is defined as $F = \{x \mid x \text{ is between } 20 \text{ and } 26\}$. In the figure, an example value 19 is fuzzified as (i.e. it is assigned the membership value) $\mu_F(19) = 0.67$

Membership functions might formally take any arbitrary form as they express only an element-wise membership condition. However, they usually exhibit smooth, monotonic shapes. This is due to the fact that membership functions are generally used to represent linguistic units described in the context of a coherent universe of discourse (i.e., the closer the elements, the more similar the characteristics they represent, as is the case for variables with physical meaning). The most commonly used membership functions are triangular, trapezoidal, and bell-shaped (see Figure 1.3).

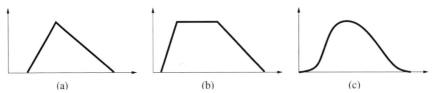

Fig. 1.3. Common membership functions. (a) triangular, (b) trapezoidal, and (c) bell-shaped.

1.2.1.2 Fuzzy Logic. As mentioned before I concentrate on the use of fuzzy rule-based systems. The rules of such a system are expressed as logical implications (i.e., in the form of **if** ... **then** statements). We can relate our previous discussion about fuzzy sets with our need for a formal basis for fuzzy logic taking advantage of the fact that "it is well established that propositional logic is isomorphic to set theory under the appropriate correspondence between components of these two mathematical systems. Furthermore, both of these systems are isomorphic to a Boolean algebra" [57]. Some of the most important equivalences between these isomorphic domains are:

Sets	Logic	Algebra
Membership	Truth	Value
Member ($\in$)	True (T)	1
Non-member ($\notin$)	False (F)	0
Intersection ($\cap$)	AND ($\vee$)	Product ($\times$)
Union ($\cup$)	OR ($\wedge$)	Sum ($+$)
Complement ($^-$)	NOT ($\sim$)	Complement ($'$)

A simple way to express this equivalence is to formulate the membership relation $x \in A$ in the form of the proposition "x is A"; e.g., *Today* $\in$ *Warm* where *Warm* $= \{x \mid x$ is between 20 and 26 degrees$\}$ is equivalent to the proposition "Today is warm". The difference between crisp and fuzzy interpretations of this proposition lies in the definition of the membership function μ_{Warm}. Indeed, referring to the crisp and fuzzy sets shown in Figures 1.1 and 1.2, respectively, and assuming that today is 19 degrees, the truth value of "Today is warm" would be respectively 0 and 0.67. Note that in the same way as fuzzy membership functions generalize the concept of crisp membership, fuzzy logic generalizes Boolean logic.

1.2.1.3 Operations. In this subsection I present the extension of the most commonly used crisp operations in the fuzzy domain. This extension imposes as a prime condition that all those fuzzy operations which are extensions of crisp concepts must reduce to their usual meaning when the fuzzy sets reduce themselves to crisp sets (i.e., when they have only **1** and **0** as membership values). In most cases there exist several possible operators satisfying this condition, some of them having a sole theoretic interest. I present below the fuzzy operators most commonly used in the frame of fuzzy inference systems. For the following definitions, assume A and B are two fuzzy subsets of U; x denotes an arbitrary element of U.

*Operators for intersection/*AND *operations* ($\mu_{A \cap B}(x) = \mu_A(x) \wedge \mu_B(x)$). Also known as t-norm operators, the most common—*minimum, product,* and *bounded product,* illustrated in Figure 1.4—are defined as follows:

$$\text{minimum} \quad : \quad \min(\mu_A(x), \mu_B(x))$$
$$\text{product} \quad : \quad \mu_A(x) \cdot \mu_B(x)$$
$$\text{bounded product} \quad : \quad \max(0, \mu_A(x) + \mu_B(x) - 1)$$

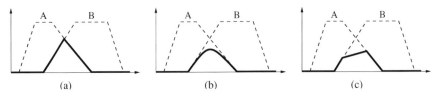

Fig. 1.4. Common t-norm (AND) operators. (a) minimum, (b) product, and (c) bounded product.

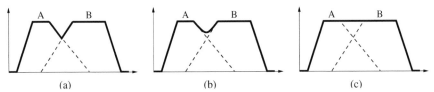

Fig. 1.5. Common t-conorm (OR) operators. (a) maximum, (b) probabilistic sum, and (c) bounded sum.

Operators for union/OR operations $(\mu_{A \cup B}(x) = \mu_A(x) \vee \mu_B(x))$. Also known as t-conorm operators, the most common—*maximum, probabilistic sum,* and *bounded sum,* exemplified in Figure 1.5—are defined as follows:

$$
\begin{aligned}
\text{maximum} \quad &: \quad \max(\mu_A(x), \mu_B(x)) \\
\text{probabilistic sum} \quad &: \quad \mu_A(x) + \mu_B(x) - \mu_A(x) \cdot \mu_B(x) \\
\text{bounded sum} \quad &: \quad \min(1, \mu_A(x) + \mu_B(x))
\end{aligned}
$$

complement/NOT operator $(\mu_{\overline{A}}(x) = \mu_{\sim A}(x))$. The so-called *fuzzy complement* operator is almost universally used in fuzzy inference systems. It is defined as follows:

$$\text{fuzzy complement} \quad : \quad 1 - \mu_A(x)$$

1.2.2 Conditional Fuzzy Statements

1.2.2.1 Linguistic Variables. In the example presented in the last section, the fuzzy set of Figure 1.2 was used to represent the concept *Warm,* referring to the day's temperature. We can also propose fuzzy sets to represent *Cold* and *Hot.* Temperature is then called a *linguistic variable,* while *Warm, Cold,* and *Hot* are their possible *linguistic values.*

The concept of linguistic variable was introduced and formalized by Zadeh [124]. A linguistic variable, also called *fuzzy variable,* is characterized by its name tag, a set of linguistic values (also known as *fuzzy values* or *labels*), and the membership functions of these labels. Figure 1.6 shows the linguistic variable *Temperature* mentioned above.

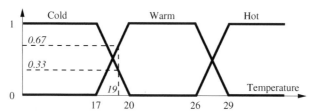

Fig. 1.6. Example of a linguistic variable: *Temperature* has three possible linguistic values, labeled *Cold*, *Warm*, and *Hot*, plotted above as degree of membership versus input value. In the figure, the example input value 19 degrees is assigned the membership values $\mu_{\text{Cold}}(19) = 0.33$, $\mu_{\text{Warm}}(19) = 0.67$, and $\mu_{\text{Hot}}(19) = 0$.

1.2.2.2 Fuzzy Conditions. As mentioned before, a proposition like "Today is warm" is assigned a truth value according to the membership function characterizing the fuzzy value *Warm*. This proposition is called *conditional fuzzy statement* or *fuzzy condition*. However, fuzzy inference systems rarely depend on a single variable to define their state. Instead of that, sentences of the type "Today is warm and partially sunny" are commonly used. Such a double fuzzy condition receives as truth value the result of the AND operation of the two single fuzzy conditions "Today is warm" and "Today is partially sunny". This corresponds to the Cartesian product of the fuzzy sets *Warm* and *Partially Sunny*, defined for the variables *Temperature* and *Sunshine* respectively. Figure 1.7 shows the bidimensional membership function characterizing the fuzzy condition "Today is warm and partially sunny". Note that fuzzy conditions can also be constructed using OR and NOT operators (e.g., "Today is hot or not cloudy").

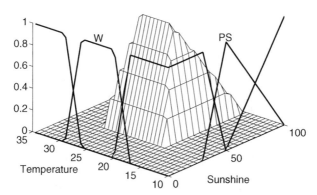

Fig. 1.7. Bidimensional membership function. The fuzzy condition "Today is warm and partially sunny" is characterized by the AND operation—the minimum operator in this case—applied on the fuzzy values *Warm (W)* and *Partially Sunny (PS)* of variables *Temperature* and *Sunshine* respectively.

1.2.3 Fuzzy Inference

To infer is defined as "to conclude from facts and reasoning". This definition presents three elements of the inference process: facts, the raw material; reasoning, the transformation engine; and conclusions, the final product. However it lacks a fourth element: knowledge, the fuel feeding the inference engine. In fuzzy inference, these four elements are also present: fuzzy facts are transformed in fuzzy conclusions by a fuzzy reasoning mechanism; knowledge is represented by fuzzy rules. This section describes three processes participating in the fuzzy reasoning mechanism: implication, aggregation, and defuzzification.

1.2.3.1 Implication. In a fuzzy inference system , the fuzzy rules have the form:

if (*input fuzzy condition*) **then** (*output fuzzy assignment*),

where *output fuzzy assignment* designates a fuzzy value resulting from applying a *causal implication* operator to the input and output fuzzy sets. The term causal implication, also known as *engineering implication* [57], refers to the fact that it preserves cause-effect relationships. The input condition and the output assignment are called, respectively *antecedent* and *consequent*. To understand the concept of causal implication, let us define the rule

if u **is** A **then** v **is** C,

where $u \in U$ and $v \in V$ (U and V are, respectively, the input and output universes of discourse). The implication operation $A \to C$ for a given input value x is characterized by the fuzzy set $C' = \mu_{A \to C}(x)$ defined on the output universe V. The most commonly used implication operators, *minimum* and *product*, are defined as follows (Figure 1.8 illustrates these operators):

$$\text{minimum} \quad C' = \quad \min(\mu_A(x), C)$$
$$\text{product} \quad C' = \quad \mu_A(x) \cdot C$$

A rule that does not fire, i.e., whose antecedent is absolutely false ($\mu_A(x) = 0$), produces an empty implication. Consequently, this rule does not participate in the inference of the whole system.

1.2.3.2 Aggregation. The rules of a fuzzy inference system are related by an *also* connective, which implies that all the rules are evaluated. Due to the overlap between fuzzy values, several rules might fire simultaneously with different truth levels, each proposing an output fuzzy set. In general, fuzzy systems are expected to propose a single decision instead of a number of different fuzzy sets. To solve this, these fuzzy sets are integrated, by means of an *aggregation* operation, to obtain a single fuzzy set that describes the output of the fuzzy system. Generally, t-conorms (i.e., OR operators) are used as aggregation operators. Figure 1.9 illustrates the aggregation operation and shows its results using maximum and bounded-sum operators.

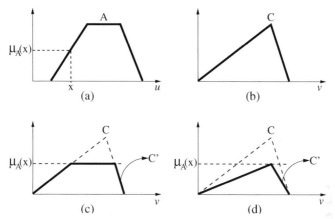

Fig. 1.8. Common implication operators. Given the rule "**if** u is A **then** v is C", the figure shows: (a) the input fuzzy value (antecedent) A with a given input element x, (b) the output fuzzy value (consequent) C, and the resulting implication $C' = \mu_{A \to C}(x)$ applying (c) minimum and (d) product implication operators.

1.2.3.3 Defuzzification. Although a single output fuzzy set—as that obtained by aggregating rule outputs—contains useful qualitative information, most of the time the output of a fuzzy system must be a crisp value. The process that produces a crisp output from a fuzzy set is called *defuzzification*. Many defuzzification methods have been proposed in the literature; however, the two most commonly used methods are the *Center of Areas (COA)*, also called center of gravity or centroid, and the *Mean of Maxima (MOM)*. Following, I define these two methods, whose results are exemplified in Figure 1.10.

Given an output fuzzy set $Y = \mu_Y(v)$ defined in the universe V of the variable v, the defuzzified output y is given by the expressions:

Center of Areas COA

$$y_{\text{COA}} = \frac{\int_V v \cdot \mu_Y(v)\, dv}{\int_V \mu_Y(v)\, dv}$$

If the output universe V is discrete, the integral expressions are replaced by the corresponding sums:

$$y_{\text{COA}} = \frac{\sum_V v \cdot \mu_Y(v)}{\sum_V \mu_Y(v)}$$

Mean of Maxima MOM

$$y_{\text{inf}} = \min(z \mid \mu_Y(z) = \max(\mu_Y(v)))$$
$$y_{\text{sup}} = \max(z \mid \mu_Y(z) = \max(\mu_Y(v)))$$
$$y_{\text{MOM}} = \frac{y_{inf} + y_{sup}}{2}$$

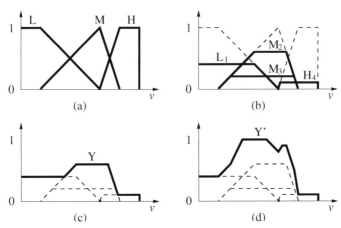

(a)

(b)

(c)

(d)

Fig. 1.9. Aggregation operation. The output variable v of a system has three fuzzy values, L, M, and H, presented in (a). In a given instant, four fuzzy rules are fired with activation levels of 0.4, 0.6, 0.2, and 0.1, producing the fuzzy sets L_1, M_2, M_3, and H_4, respectively, as shown in (b). The aggregation operation integrates these fuzzy sets applying a t-conorm operator at each point of the output universe. The figure shows the resulting fuzzy sets when using maximum (c) and bounded-sum (d) operators. Note that the latter operator ascribes greater importance to the number of active rules with identical (or similar) consequent than the former does.

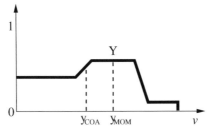

Fig. 1.10. Defuzzification. This process produces a crisp value y from a given fuzzy set Y. The figure shows the resulting values obtained using two common methods: y_{COA} for the Center of Areas and y_{MOM} for the Mean of Maxima.

1.2.4 Fuzzy Inference Systems

Generally speaking, the term fuzzy system applies to any system whose operation is mainly based on fuzzy theory concepts such as reasoning, arithmetic, algebra, topology, or programming, among others. However, in the frame of this book I use the terms fuzzy inference system and fuzzy system to design a rule-based system that uses: (1) linguistic variables, (2) fuzzy sets to represent the linguistic values of such variables, (3) fuzzy rules to describe causal relationships between them, and (4) fuzzy inference to compute the response of the system to a given input.

1.2.4.1 General Structure. The basic structure of a fuzzy system consists of four main components, as depicted in Figure 1.11: (1) a knowledge base, which contains both an ensemble of fuzzy rules, known as the rule base, and an ensemble of membership functions known as the database; (2) a fuzzifier, which translates crisp inputs into fuzzy values; (3) an inference engine that applies a fuzzy reasoning mechanism to obtain a fuzzy output; and (4) a defuzzifier, which translates this latter output into a crisp value. These components perform the aforementioned processes necessary to fuzzy inference.

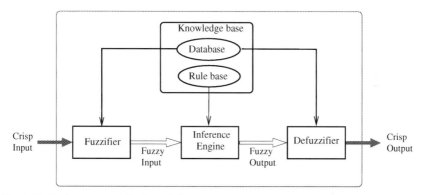

Fig. 1.11. Basic structure of a fuzzy inference system.

Below, I illustrate the functioning of a fuzzy inference system by means of a simple example.

The tourist prediction system. A simple fuzzy system is proposed to predict the number of tourists visiting a resort (for more details on building fuzzy systems, see Section 2.1). The prediction is based on two weather-related input variables: (1) the temperature, measured in degrees and (2) the sunshine, expressed as a percentage of the maximum expected sunshine. The system outputs an estimated amount of tourists expressed in terms of percentage of the resort's capacity. The example presented here is developed for a slightly cold, partially sunny day: the observed temperature and sunshine are 19 degrees and 60%, respectively.

Knowledge base. The knowledge describing the system's behavior is represented by the membership functions defining the linguistic variables (the "database" unit in Figure 1.11) and by a set of rules (the "rule-base" unit in figure 1.11).

Database. Three linguistic variables are defined. Two inputs: *Temperature*, and *Sunshine*, and one output: *Tourists*. Each variable has three membership functions: *Cold*, *Warm*, and *Hot* for the first input, *Cloudy*, *Partially Sunny*, and *Sunny* for the second input, and *Low*, *Medium*, and *High* for the output. Figure 1.12 shows these variables.

Rule base. The following three rules describe the behavior of the prediction system:

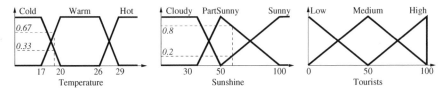

Fig. 1.12. Tourist prediction example: database. The three variables *Temperature*, *Sunshine*, and *Tourists* have three membership functions each one. The figure shows the fuzzification of two given input values: 19 degrees for *Temperature* and 60% for *Sunshine*.

Rule 1:   **if** (*Temperature* **is** *Hot*) **or** (*Sunshine* **is** *Sunny*) **then** (*Tourists* **is** *High*)

Rule 2:   **if** (*Temperature* **is** *Warm*) **and** (*Sunshine* **is** *Partially Sunny*) **then** (*Tourists* **is** *Medium*)

Rule 3:   **if** (*Temperature* **is** *Cold*) **or** (*Sunshine* **is** *Cloudy*) **then** (*Tourists* **is** *Low*)

Fuzzifier. This unit computes the membership values of each input variable in accordance with the fuzzy values defined in the database (see Figure 1.12).

Temperature			Sunshine		
$\mu_{Cold}(19)$	$=$	$0.33,$	$\mu_{Cloudy}(60)$	$=$	$0,$
$\mu_{Warm}(19)$	$=$	$0.67,$	$\mu_{PartSunny}(60)$	$=$	$0.8,$
$\mu_{Hot}(19)$	$=$	$0.$	$\mu_{Sunny}(60)$	$=$	$0.2.$

Inference engine. This unit interprets the rules contained in the rule base. The inference is performed in three steps: (1) antecedent activation, (2) implication, and (3) aggregation.

Antecedent activation. The inference engine takes the membership values of the input fuzzy conditions of each rule—computed previously by the fuzzifier—and then applies the fuzzy operators indicated to obtain the rule's truth level.

Rule 1: **if** (*Temperature* **is** *Hot*) **or** (*Sunshine* **is** *Sunny*)

$$
\begin{aligned}
\mu_{Rule\ 1} &= \mu_{Hot}(19) \vee \mu_{Sunny}(60) \\
&= \max(0, 0.2) \\
&= 0.2
\end{aligned}
$$

Rule 2: **if** (*Temperature* **is** *Warm*) **and** (*Sunshine* **is** *Partially Sunny*)

$$
\begin{aligned}
\mu_{Rule\ 2} &= \mu_{Warm}(19) \wedge \mu_{PartSunny}(60) \\
&= \min(0.67, 0.8) \\
&= 0.67
\end{aligned}
$$

Rule 3: **if** (*Temperature* **is** *Cold*) **or** (*Sunshine* **is** *Cloudy*)

$$\begin{aligned} \mu_{\text{Rule 3}} &= \mu_{\text{Cold}}(19) \vee \mu_{\text{Cloudy}}(60) \\ &= \max(0.33, 0) \\ &= 0.33 \end{aligned}$$

Implication. The inference engine then applies the implication operator to each rule in order to obtain the fuzzy output values. In this example, I apply the *minimum* implication operator. Figure 1.13 shows the fuzzy sets resulting from this operation.

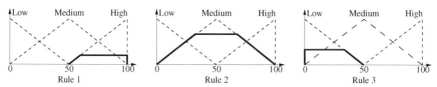

Fig. 1.13. Tourist prediction example: implication. The inference engine applies the *minimum* implication operator to each rule in order to obtain the fuzzy output values. Rule truth values are respectively $\mu_{\text{Rule 1}} = 0.2$, $\mu_{\text{Rule 2}} = 0.67$, and $\mu_{\text{Rule 3}} = 0.33$.

Aggregation. Finally, the inference engine aggregates the three fuzzy sets obtained in the implication stage in a single fuzzy output. In this example, I apply *maximum* as aggregation operator. Figure 1.14 shows the fuzzy set resulting of this operation.

Defuzzifier. As mentioned before, an output fuzzy set as that shown in Figure 1.14 carries important qualitative information. However, the tourist prediction problem requires a crisp value quantifying the expected percentage of tourists. The defuzzifier of this example computes this value applying the COA defuzzification method (Section 1.2.3). The output of the tourist prediction system for the given input conditions—i.e. a temperature of 19 degrees and a sunshine of 60%—is thus approximately 48%.

The fuzzy system presented above, can be seen as a 2-input, 1-output block as that shown in Figure 1.15

1.2.4.2 Types of Fuzzy Systems. There exists three main types of fuzzy systems that differ in the way they define the consequents of their rules: Mamdani, TSK, and Singleton fuzzy systems. I sketch below their main characteristics:

Mamdani fuzzy systems. These fuzzy systems have fuzzy sets as rule consequents, as those presented in this section. They are called Mamdani fuzzy systems as they were first proposed by Mamdani [53,54]. Their main advantage is high interpretability, due to the fact that output variables are defined linguistically and each rule consequent takes on a value from a set of labels with associated meaning. However, they also have some drawbacks, among which the most important are their lack of accuracy and their high computational cost. The accuracy of the system is usually

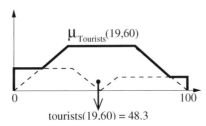

Fig. 1.14. Tourist prediction example: aggregation and defuzzification. Aggregation integrates the fuzzy sets of Figure 1.13 into a single output fuzzy set. This fuzzy set, called here $\mu_{\text{Tourists}}(19, 60)$, represents the fuzzy (qualitative) prediction of the expected amount of tourists. The defuzzification process translates the output fuzzy value, $\mu_{\text{Tourists}}(19, 60)$, into a crisp value, Tourists$(19, 60)$, quantifying this expected amount. In this example, the final output value is approximately 48%.

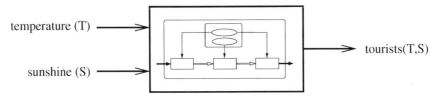

Fig. 1.15. Tourist prediction example: input-output block representation. The tourist-prediction block has two inputs—temperature (T) and sunshine (S)—and one output—tourists(T, S).

limited by the rigidity of linguistic values. The high computational cost is related to the operations required to compute the center of areas of the fuzzy sets, i.e., two integrals or sums and one division for each inference.

TSK fuzzy systems. These systems derive their name from Takagi, Sugeno, and Kang who proposed an alternative type of fuzzy systems [106, 108], in which the consequent of each fuzzy rule is represented by a function—usually linear—of the input variables. Thanks to their functional description, TSK-type systems usually exhibit greater accuracy than Mamdani systems. However, the interpretability of their rules is significantly reduced as they no longer represent linguistic concepts.

Coming back to the tourist-prediction example, we can convert the system into a TSK system by replacing the three linguistic consequents—*Low*, *Medium*, and *High*—with carefully calculated, corresponding linear functions of the input variables. The three rule consequents thus become:

Rule 1: **if** ... **then** *Tourists* $= f_1(T, S) = 2T + 0.8S - 40$
Rule 2: **if** ... **then** *Tourists* $= f_2(T, S) = T + S - 23$
Rule 3: **if** ... **then** *Tourists* $= f_3(T, S) = 0.5T + 0.3S$

With this consequents, the implication step propose the following predictions:

	Rule 1	Rule 2	Rule 3
Truth level (μ_{Rule})	0.2	0.67	0.33
Estimated tourists	$f_1(19, 60) = 46\%$	$f_2(19, 60) = 56\%$	$f_3(19, 60) = 27.5\%$

The aggregation step does not modify these values. Then, the defuzzifier receives this discrete output set to produce the following output:

$$
\begin{aligned}
\text{tourists}(19,60) &= \frac{\sum_{i=1}^{3} f_i(19,60) \cdot \mu_{\text{Rule } i}}{\sum_{i=1}^{3} \mu_{\text{Rule } i}} \\
&= \frac{0.2 \times 46\% + 0.67 \times 56\% + 0.33 \times 27.5\%}{0.2 + 0.67 + 0.33} \\
&= 46.4\%
\end{aligned}
$$

Singleton fuzzy systems. The rule consequents of this type of systems are constant values. Singleton fuzzy systems can be considered as a particular case of either Mamdani or TSK fuzzy systems. In fact, a constant value is equivalent to both a singleton fuzzy set—i.e., a fuzzy set that concentrates its membership value in a single point of the universe—and a linear function in which the coefficients of the input variables value **0**. The singleton representation constitutes a trade-off between the interpretability offered by Mamdani systems with their meaningful labels and the accuracy provided by TSK systems with their linear functions. Moreover, thanks to the discrete representation of the output variable, the defuzzification process demands less computation than in the other two cases.

In the tourist-prediction example, the Mamdani-type system is easily converted into a singleton-type system replacing the fuzzy values *Low*, *Medium*, and *High* for their corresponding center of areas: 0%, 50%, and 100%. With these new consequents, the implication step propose thus:

	Rule 1	Rule 2	Rule 3
Truth level (μ_{Rule})	0.2	0.67	0.33
Estimated tourists	High $= 100\%$	Medium $= 50\%$	Low $= 0\%$

that is defuzzified as follows:

$$
\begin{aligned}
\text{tourists}(19,60) &= \frac{\sum_{i=1}^{3} f_i(19,60) \cdot \mu_{\text{Rule } i}}{\sum_{i=1}^{3} \mu_{\text{Rule } i}} \\
&= \frac{0.2 \times 100\% + 0.67 \times 50\% + 0.33 \times 0\%}{0.2 + 0.67 + 0.33} \\
&= 44.4\%
\end{aligned}
$$

1.2.4.3 Connectionist Representation. Several authors [40, 50] have used an alternative representation of fuzzy systems, similar to connectionist models, in which the elements of the fuzzy system are represented by functional blocks connected according to the knowledge contained in the system and usually organized in five layers representing different steps of the reasoning process. The five steps represented by the layers are: fuzzification (membership functions), antecedent activation (logical operators), implication, aggregation, and defuzzification.

To illustrate this representation, Figure 1.16 shows the connectionist model of the tourist-prediction system.

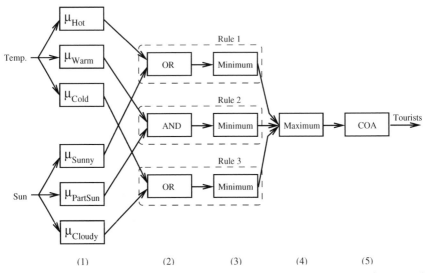

Fig. 1.16. Tourist prediction example: connectionist representation. Five layers of connected functional blocks represent the steps and the elements of the fuzzy inference process: (1) fuzzification (membership functions), (2) antecedent activation (logical operators), (3) implication, (4) aggregation, and (5) defuzzification.

1.3 Evolutionary Computation

The domain of evolutionary computation involves the study of the foundations and the applications of computational techniques based on the principles of natural evolution. Evolution in nature is responsible for the "design" of all living beings on earth, and for the strategies they use to interact with each other. Evolutionary algorithms employ this powerful design philosophy to find solutions to hard problems.

Generally speaking, evolutionary techniques can be viewed either as search methods, or as optimization techniques. As written by Michalewicz [60]: "Any abstract task to be accomplished can be thought of as solving a problem, which, in turn, can be perceived as a search through a space of potential solutions. Since usually we are after 'the best' solution, we can view this task as an optimization process."

The first works on the use of evolution-inspired approaches to problem solving date back to the late 1950s [7, 8, 22, 26, 27]. Independent and almost simultaneous research conducted by Rechenberg and Schwefel on *evolution strategies* [91, 92, 98, 99], by Holland on *genetic algorithms* [32, 34], and by Fogel on *evolutionary programming* [24, 25] triggered the study and the application of evolutionary techniques.

Three basic mechanisms drive natural evolution: *reproduction, mutation,* and *selection.* These mechanisms act on the *chromosomes* containing the genetic information of the *individual* (the *genotype*), rather than on the individual itself (the *phenotype*). Reproduction is the process whereby new individuals are introduced into a *population.* During sexual reproduction, *recombination* (or *crossover*) occurs, transmitting to the offspring chromosomes that are a melange of both parents' genetic information. Mutation introduces small changes into the inherited chromosomes; it often results from copying errors during reproduction. Selection is a process guided by the Darwinian principle of survival of the fittest. The fittest individuals are those best adapted to their environment, which thus survive and reproduce.

Evolutionary computation makes use of a metaphor of natural evolution. According to this metaphor, a problem plays the role of an environment wherein lives a population of individuals, each representing a possible solution to the problem. The degree of adaptation of each individual (i.e., candidate solution) to its environment is expressed by an adequacy measure known as the *fitness function*. The phenotype of each individual, i.e., the candidate solution itself, is generally encoded in some manner into its *genome* (genotype). Like evolution in nature, evolutionary algorithms potentially produce progressively better solutions to the problem. This is possible thanks to the constant introduction of new "genetic" material into the population, by applying so-called genetic operators that are the computational equivalents of natural evolutionary mechanisms.

There are several types of evolutionary algorithms, among which the best known are *genetic algorithms*, *genetic programming*, *evolution strategies*, and *evolutionary programming*; though different in the specifics they are all based on the same general principles. The archetypal evolutionary algorithm proceeds as follows: An initial population of individuals, $P(0)$, is generated at random or heuristically. Every evolutionary step t, known as a *generation*, the individuals in the current population, $P(t)$, are *decoded* and *evaluated* according to some predefined quality criterion, referred to as the fitness, or fitness function. Then, a subset of individuals, $P'(t)$—known as the *mating pool*—is selected to reproduce, with selection of individuals done according to their fitness. Thus, high-fitness ("good") individuals stand a better chance of "reproducing," while low-fitness ones are more likely to disappear.

Selection alone cannot introduce any new individuals into the population, i.e., it cannot find new points in the search space. These points are generated by altering the selected population $P'(t)$ via the application of crossover and mutation, so as to produce a new population, $P''(t)$. Crossover tends to enable the evolutionary process to move toward "promising" regions of the search space. Mutation is introduced to prevent premature convergence to local optima, by randomly sampling new points in the search space. Finally, the new individuals $P''(t)$ are introduced into the next-generation population, $P(t + 1)$; although a part of $P(t)$ can be preserved, usually $P''(t)$ simply becomes $P(t + 1)$. The termination condition may be specified as some fixed, maximal number of generations or as the attainment of an acceptable fitness level. Figure 1.17 presents the structure of a generic evolutionary algorithm in pseudo-code format.

Evolutionary techniques exhibit a number of advantages over other search methods as they combine elements of directed and stochastic search. First, they usually need a smaller amount of knowledge and fewer assumptions about the characteristics of the search space. Second, they can more easily avoid getting stuck in local optima. Finally, they strike a good balance between *exploitation* of the best solu-

```
begin EA
    t:=0
    Initialize population P(t)
    while not done do
        Evaluate P(t)
        P'(t) = Select[P(t)]
        P''(t) = ApplyGeneticOperators[P'(t)]
        P(t + 1) = Merge[P''(t),P(t)]
        t:=t+1
    end while
end EA
```

Fig. 1.17. Pseudo-code of an evolutionary algorithm.

tions, and *exploration* of the search space. The strength of evolutionary algorithms relies on their population-based search, and on the use of the genetic mechanisms described above. The existence of a population of candidate solutions entails a parallel search, with the selection mechanism directing the search to the most promising regions. The crossover operator encourages the exchange of information between these search-space regions, while the mutation operator enables the exploration of new directions.

The application of an evolutionary algorithm involves a number of important considerations. The first decision to take when applying such an algorithm is how to encode candidate solutions within the genome. The representation must allow for the encoding of all possible solutions while being sufficiently simple to be searched in a reasonable amount of time. Next, an appropriate fitness function must be defined for evaluating the individuals. The (usually scalar) fitness must reflect the criteria to be optimized and their relative importance. Representation and fitness are thus clearly problem-dependent, in contrast to selection, crossover, and mutation, which seem *prima facie* more problem-independent. Practice has shown, however, that while standard genetic operators can be used, one often needs to tailor these to the problem as well.

We noted above that there are several types of evolutionary algorithms. This classification is due mainly to historical reasons and the different types of evolutionary algorithms are in fact quite similar. One could argue that there is but a single general evolutionary algorithm, or just the opposite–that "there are as many evolutionary algorithms as the researchers working in evolutionary computation" [83]. The frontiers among the widely accepted classes of evolutionary algorithms have become fuzzy over the years as each technique has attempted to overcome its limitations, by imbibing characteristics of the other techniques. To design an evolutionary algorithm one must define a number of important parameters, which are precisely those that demarcate the different evolutionary-computation classes. Some important parameters are: representation (genome), selection mechanism, crossover, mutation, size of populations P' and P'', variability or fixity of population size, and variability or fixity of genome length.

The rest of this chapter presents the major evolutionary methods, emphasizing the specific properties of each one along with the most typical choices of parameters. These methods are: Genetic algorithms (Section 1.3.1), genetic programming (Section 1.3.2), evolution strategies (Section 1.3.3), and evolutionary programming (Section 1.3.4). Finally, Section 1.3.5 introduces a somewhat different evolutionary technique, known as *classifier systems*, which offers on-line learning capabilities. A detailed discussion on theory and on advanced topics of evolutionary computation, which is available in many books [2, 60, 61, 109, 113], goes beyond the reach of this chapter.

1.3.1 Genetic Algorithms

Proposed by John Holland in the 1960s [32, 34], genetic algorithms are the best known class of evolutionary algorithms. They are used so extensively that often the terms genetic algorithms and evolutionary computation are used interchangeably (though, as noted, they should be considered distinct).

There is a clear distinction between the solution being tested, the "adult individual" or phenotype, and its representation—the genome or genotype. Traditionally, the genome is a fixed-length binary string. With such a data structure it is possible to represent solutions to virtually any problem. However, so that the genetic algorithm may converge to good solutions, the representation must be carefully designed to minimize redundancy (i.e., several genotypes encoding the same phenotype) and to avoid invalid representations (i.e., a genotype encoding a phenotype which is not a possible solution to the problem at hand).

With genetic algorithms, the population size is constant and individuals are decoded and evaluated at each generation. Individuals are then selected according to their fitness. Many selection procedures are currently in use, one of the simplest being *fitness-proportionate selection*, where individuals are selected with a probability proportional to their fitness. This ensures that the expected number of times an individual is chosen is approximately proportional to its relative performance in the population. Selection produces a mating pool of the same size as the original population ($\|P'\| = \|P\|$).

Crossover is performed with probability p_c (the "crossover probability" or "crossover rate") between two selected individuals, called *parents*, by exchanging parts of their genomes to form two new individuals, called *offspring*. In its simplest form, known as *one-point crossover*, substrings are exchanged after a randomly selected crossover point. The mutation operator is carried out by flipping bits at random, with some (usually small) probability p_m. The crossover and mutation operators preserve the size of the population, i.e., $\|P''\| = \|P'\|$.

Genetic algorithms are by far the most popular evolutionary technique (though genetic programming is rapidly "gaining" on them). This is due in part to their conceptual simplicity, the ease of programming entailed, and the small number of parameters to be defined (apart from the genomic representation and the fitness function, parameters include mainly population size, crossover and mutation probabilities, and termination condition).

There are several variations of the simple genetic algorithm [113], with different selection mechanisms (e.g., *ranking, tournament,* and *elitism*), crossover operators (e.g., *multi-point crossover*), and mutation operators (e.g., *adaptive mutation*). There exist a profusion of books concerning these and other advanced topics related with genetic algorithms [60, 61, 113].

1.3.2 Genetic Programming

John Koza developed a variant of genetic algorithms called genetic programming [48, 49]. In this approach, instead of encoding possible solutions to a problem as a fixed-length character string, they are encoded as computer programs. To wit, the individuals in the population are programs that— when executed—are the candidate solutions (phenotypes) to the problem.

Programs in genetic programming may be expressed in any language in principle. However, to guarantee that evolution be able to generate valid, executable programs, it is necessary to restrict the choice of language. Thus, programs are expressed as parse trees, rather than as lines of code, i.e., using a functional language rather than a procedural one. The set of possible internal (non-terminal) nodes of these parse trees, called the *function set (F)*, is composed of user-defined functions. The terminal nodes, which form the *terminal set (T)*, are usually either variables or constants. The *syntactic closure* property requires that each function in F be able to accept as arguments any other returned function value and any value and data type in the terminal set T. This property prevents the proliferation of illegal programs due to crossover and mutation. As an example consider a basic arithmetic language whose function and terminal set are defined as follows: $F = \{+, -, *, /\}$ and $T = \{A, B, C, 2\}$. Figure 1.18 shows two examples of parse trees.

Evolution in genetic programming proceeds along the general lines of the generic evolutionary algorithm (Figure 1.17), with the genetic operators adapted to the tree representation. Reproduction is performed in both asexual and sexual ways. Asexual reproduction, or *cloning*, allows some of the fittest individuals to survive into the next generation; this is equivalent to so-called elitist selection in genetic algorithms. Sexual reproduction, i.e., crossover, starts out by selecting a random crossover point in each parent tree and then exchanging the subtrees "hanging" from these points, thus producing two offspring trees (Figure 1.19). Mutation in genetic programming is considered as a secondary genetic operator and is applied much less frequently [49]. It is performed by removing a subtree at a randomly selected point and inserting at that point a new random subtree.

One important issue in genetic programming is related to the size of the trees. Under the influence of the crossover operator, the depth of the trees can quickly increase, leading to a fitness plateau. The presence of huge programs in the population also has direct consequences vis-a-vis computer memory and evaluation speed. Most implementations of genetic programming include mechanisms to prevent trees from becoming too deep. However, these mechanisms also present a disadvantage, in that they reduce the genetic diversity contained in larger trees. There exist a num-

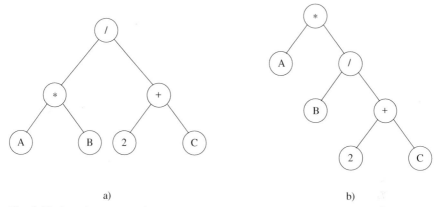

a)   b)

Fig. 1.18. Genetic programming parse trees, representing the following programs in LISP-like syntax: a) $(/(*AB)(+2C))$ and b) $(*A(/B(+2C)))$. Both programs implement the expression $AB/(2+C)$. It is important to note that though LISP is the language chosen by Koza to implement genetic programming, it is not the only possibility. Any language capable of representing programs as parse trees is adequate. Moreover, machine language has been used as well [69].

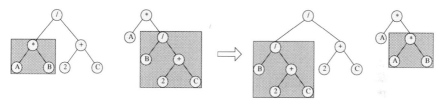

Fig. 1.19. Crossover in genetic programming. The two shadowed subtrees of the parent trees are exchanged to produce two offspring trees. Note that the two parents, as well as the two offspring, are typically of different size.

ber of books consacred to other advanced topics and applications of genetic programming, which is a field in constant expansion [3].

1.3.3 Evolution Strategies

Evolution strategies were introduced by Ingo Rechenberg [91, 92] and Hans-Paul Schweffel [98, 99] in the 1960s as a method for solving parameter-optimization problems. In its most general form the phenotype of an individual is a vector x containing the candidate values of the parameters being optimized. The genotype of each individual is a pair of real-valued vectors $v = \{x, \sigma\}$, where x is the above phenotypic vector (the genotype-phenotype distinction is thus somewhat degenerate with evolution strategies), and σ is a vector of standard deviations used to apply the mutation operator. The inclusion of the σ vector in the genome allows the algorithm to *self-adapt* the mutation operator while searching for the solution.

Somewhat different than the generic evolutionary algorithm (Figure 1.17), selection is performed *after* the genetic operators have been applied. The standard notations in this domain, (μ,λ)–ES and $(\mu + \lambda)$–ES, denote algorithms in which a population of μ parents generates λ offspring. The next generation is created by selecting the fittest μ individuals. In the case of (μ,λ)–ES only the λ offspring are considered for selection, thus limiting the "life" of an individual to one generation, while in the $(\mu + \lambda)$–ES the μ parents are also considered for selection.

Mutation is the major genetic operator in evolution strategies. It also plays the role of a reproduction operator given that the mutated individual is viewed as an offspring for the selection operator to work on. In its most general form, mutation modifies a genotype $v = \{x,\sigma\}$ by first randomly altering σ, and then modifying x according to the new values provided by σ. This operation produces a new individual $v' = \{x',\sigma'\}$, where $x' = x + N(0,\sigma')$. $N(0,\sigma')$ denotes a vector of independent random Gaussian values with mean 0 and standard deviations σ'.

The crossover (or recombination) operator generates an offspring from a number of parents (usually two). There are two types of crossover operators: discrete and intermediate. In discrete recombination each component of v, i.e., each pair of scalars (x_i,σ_i), is copied from one of the parents at random. In intermediate recombination, the offspring values are a linear combination of all the parent vectors participating in the recombination process.

The earliest evolution strategies were (1+1)–ES [91, 98], involving a single parent–single offspring search. Mutation was the only genetic operator, and the standard deviation vector σ was constant or modified by some deterministic algorithm. Later, recombination was added as evolution strategies were extended to encompass populations of individuals.

A good source for further information on evolution strategies is the book by Schwefel [100].

1.3.4 Evolutionary Programming

Lawrence Fogel proposed evolutionary programming [24, 25] as a means to develop artificial intelligence. He argued that intelligent behavior requires both the ability to predict changes in an environment, and a translation of the predictions into actions appropriate for reaching a goal. In its most general, the environment is described as a sequence of symbols taken from a finite alphabet. With its knowledge of the environment the evolving entity is supposed to produce an output symbol that is related in some way to the next symbol appearing in the environment. The output symbol should maximize a *payoff function*, which measures the accuracy of the prediction. *Finite state machines* were selected to represent individuals in evolutionary programming as they provide a meaningful representation of behavior based on interpretation of symbols.

A finite state machine is a machine possessing a finite number of different internal states. When stimulated by an input symbol the machine undergoes a transition (i.e., a change in the internal state) and produces an output symbol. The behavior of the finite state machine is described completely by defining the *(output symbol,next state)* pair for each *(input symbol,current state)* pair. Figure 1.20 shows an example of a three-state machine.

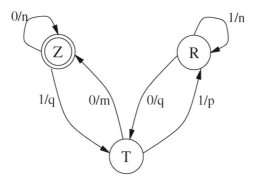

Fig. 1.20. A finite state machine with states $\{Z, T, R\}$. The input symbols belong to the set $\{0, 1\}$, whereas the output alphabet is the set $\{m, n, p, q\}$. The edges representing the state transitions are labeled a/b, where a represents the input symbol triggering the transition, and b represents the output symbol. For example, when the machine is in state R and the input is 0 it switches to state T and outputs q. A double circle indicates the initial state.

Evolutionary programming maintains a population of finite state machines, each one representing a particular candidate behavior for solving the problem at hand. The fitness of an individual is calculated by presenting sequentially to the finite state machine the symbols in the environment and observing the predicted output. The quality of the prediction is quantified according to the given payoff function. Once the individual has been exposed to the whole sequence of symbols, its overall performance (e.g., average payoff per symbol) is used as the fitness value.

Like with evolution strategies, evolutionary programming first generates offspring and then selects the next generation. There is no sexual reproduction (crossover), but rather each parent machine is mutated to produce a single offspring. There are five possible mutation operators: change of an output symbol, change of a state transition, addition of a state, deletion of a state, and change of the initial state. The two latter operations are not allowed when the parent machine has only one state. Mutation operators and the number of mutations per offspring are chosen with respect to a probability distribution. The offspring are then evaluated in the same way as their parents, and the next generation is selected from the ensemble of parents and offspring. This process is iterated until a new symbol is required in the environment. The best individual obtained up to this moment provides the prediction, the new symbol is added to the environment, and the algorithm is executed again. Note that as opposed to most evolutionary-computation applications where fitness is fixed from the outset, evolutionary programming inherently incorporates a *dynamic* fitness, i.e., the environment changes in time. Fogel's book [23] is a good reference on evolutionary programming.

1.3.5 Classifier Systems

Classifier systems, presented by Holland [33, 34], are evolution-based learning systems, rather than a "pure" evolutionary algorithm. They can be thought of as restricted versions of classical rule-based systems, with the addition of input and output interfaces. A classifier system consists of three main components: (1) the *rule and message system*, which performs the inference and defines the behavior of the whole system, (2) the *apportionment of credit system*, which adapts the behavior by credit assignment, and (3) the genetic algorithm, which adapts the system's knowledge by rule discovery.

The rule and message system includes four subcomponents: the *message list*, the *classifier list*, the *input interface*, and the *output interface*. The input interface, also known as the *detector*, translates information from the system's environment into one or more finite-length binary *messages*, which are posted to the finite-length message list. These messages may then *activate* one or more matching *classifiers* from the classifier list. A classifier is a rule of the form **if** *condition* **then** *message*, where *condition* is a finite-length string , and the *message*, posted to the message list, may then activate other classifiers or trigger a system's action through the output interface, also called the *effector* (the alphabet of classifiers includes the symbol $\#$ that plays the role of a wild-card character).

The apportionment-of-credit algorithm adapts the behavior of the classifier system by modifying the way existing classifiers are used. Unlike traditional rule-based systems, classifier systems use parallel rule activation. This characteristic allows the system to accelerate the inference process and to coordinate several actions simultaneously. However, with such a competitive approach the system must determine the importance (*strength*) of rules in order to combine them to make an overall decision. Although there are several ways to accomplish this, the *bucket-brigade algorithm* continues to be the most popular [28]. It is a parallel, local, credit-assignment-based reinforcement learning algorithm, which may be viewed as an "information market," where the right to trade information is bought and sold by classifiers. Each matched classifier makes a *bid* proportional to its strength. Rules that have accumulated a large "capital" (i.e., strength) are preferred over other rules.

The genetic algorithm adapts the classifier system by introducing new classifiers (rules). There exist two approaches for the application of evolutionary techniques in the design of rule-based systems in general: the Michigan approach and the Pittsburgh approach; these two approaches are also applied to classifier systems. In the Michigan approach, each individual represents a single rule, and the classifier list is represented by the entire population. The strengths calculated by the bucket-brigade algorithm are used as fitness function to evaluate the quality of each classifier. In the Pittsburgh approach, the genetic algorithm maintains a population of candidate classifier lists, with each individual representing an entire list. A good introduction to classifier systems is given by Goldberg [28].

2 Evolutionary Fuzzy Modeling

The Merriam-Webster online dictionary (www.m-w.com) defines *model* as "a system of postulates, data, and inferences presented as a mathematical description of an entity or state of affairs." Designing models of complex real-world systems and processes is essential in many fields of science and engineering. The models developed can be used, among others, to explain the behavior of a system, to predict the system's future development, and to keep it under control.

The traditional approach to building models—known as *white-box modeling*—assumes that everything about the system is known a priori, expressed either mathematically or verbally. In another common approach—*black-box modeling*—a model is constructed entirely from data using no additional a-priori knowledge. For example, in artificial neural networks, a structure is chosen for the network and the parameters (e.g., the connection weights and threshold values) are tuned to fit the observed data as best as possible. Such parameters are not human-interpretable and do not offer any insight about the modeled system.

A third, intermediate approach, called *grey-box modeling* [51], takes into account certain prior knowledge of the modeled system to provide the black-box models with human-interpretable meaning. In this way, the modeling process efficiently uses the available *a priori* knowledge and concentrates its efforts in estimating what is still unknown.

Fuzzy modeling techniques, namely, the construction of fuzzy rule-based inference systems, can be viewed as grey-box modeling because they allow the modeler to *extract and interpret* the knowledge contained in the model, as well as to imbue it with a-priori knowledge. However, the construction of fuzzy models of large and complex systems—with a large number of intricately related input and output variables—is a hard task demanding the identification of many parameters. One way to solve this problem is to use a nature-inspired method: evolution.

In this chapter, section 2.1 provides an overview of fuzzy modeling, section 2.2 presents the application of artificial evolution to the fuzzy modeling problem, section 2.3 discusses some aspects related to interpretability requirements, and in section 2.4 a real-world problem—the Wisconsin breast cancer diagnosis (WBCD) problem—serves to illustrate the application of evolutionary fuzzy modeling.

C.A. Peña Reyes: Coevolutionary Fuzzy Modeling, LNCS 3204, pp. 27–50, 2004.
© Springer-Verlag Berlin Heidelberg 2004

2.1 Fuzzy Modeling: The Art of Building Fuzzy Systems

The principles of fuzzy modeling were outlined by Zadeh in [123] where he proposed a new approach that "provides an approximate and yet effective means of describing the behavior of systems which are too complex or too ill-defined to admit use of precise mathematical analysis." The models proposed by Zadeh present three distinguishable features: (1) the use of linguistic variables in place or in addition to numerical variables, (2) the description of simple relations between variables by conditional fuzzy statements, and (3) the characterization of complex relations by fuzzy algorithms. Current fuzzy modeling techniques still follow these principles.

An important issue in designing fuzzy models, which is a difficult and extremely ill-defined process, involves the question of providing a methodology for their development. i.e., a set of techniques for obtaining the fuzzy model from information and knowledge about the system. The next section presents some generalities about the fuzzy modeling problem, followed by a description of some approaches to solve it in section 2.1.2

2.1.1 The Fuzzy Modeling Problem

Fuzzy modeling is the task of identifying the parameters of a fuzzy inference system so that a desired behavior is attained [120]. Note that, due to linguistic and numeric requirements, the fuzzy-modeling process has generally to deal with an important trade-off between the *accuracy* and the *interpretability* of the model. In other words, the model is expected to provide high numeric precision while incurring as little a loss of linguistic descriptive power as possible. With the *direct* approach a fuzzy model is constructed using knowledge from a human expert [120]. This task becomes difficult when the available knowledge is incomplete or when the problem space is very large, thus motivating the use of *automatic* approaches to fuzzy modeling. One of the major problems in fuzzy modeling is the *curse of dimensionality*, meaning that the computation requirements grow exponentially with the number of variables.

Following the connectionist representation of a fuzzy system, presented in Figure 1.16, the parameters of a fuzzy inference system can be classified into the four categories presented below. Table 2.1, summarizes this classification.

1. **Logical parameters.** Functions and operators which define the type of transformations undergone by crisp and fuzzy quantities during the inference process. They include the shape of the membership functions, the fuzzy logic operators applied for AND, OR, implication, and aggregation operations, and the defuzzyfication method.
2. **Structural parameters.** Related mainly with the size of the fuzzy system. Includes the number of variables participating in the inference, the number of membership functions defining each linguistic variable, and the number of rules used to perform the inference.

3. **Connective parameters.** Related with the topology of the system, these parameters define the connection between the different linguistic instances. They include the antecedents, the consequents, and the weights of the rules.
4. **Operational parameters.** These parameters define the mapping between the linguistic and the numeric representations of the variables. They characterize the membership functions of the linguistic variables.

Table 2.1. Parameter classification of fuzzy inference systems.

Class	Parameters
Logical	Reasoning mechanism
	Fuzzy operators
	Membership function types
	Defuzzification method
Structural	Relevant variables
	Number of membership functions
	Number of rules
Connective	Antecedents of rules
	Consequents of rules
	Rule weights
Operational	Membership function values

In fuzzy modeling, logical parameters are usually predefined by the designer based on experience and on problem characteristics. Typical choices for the reasoning mechanism are Mamdani-type, Takagi-Sugeno-Kang (TSK)-type, and singleton-type (Section 1.2.4) [120]. Common fuzzy operators are *minimum*, *maximum*, *product*, *bounded product*, *bounded sum*, and *probabilistic sum*(Section 1.2.1. The most common membership functions are triangular, trapezoidal, and bell-shaped. As for defuzzification, several methods have been proposed with the Center Of Area (COA) and the Mean Of Maxima (MOM) being the most popular [57, 120] (Section 1.2.3).

Structural, connective, and operational parameters may be either predefined, or obtained by synthesis or search methodologies. Generally, the search space, and thus the computational effort, grows exponentially with the number of parameters. Therefore, one can either invest more resources in the chosen search methodology, or infuse more *a priori*, expert knowledge into the system (thereby effectively reducing the search space). The aforementioned trade-off between accuracy and interpretability is usually expressed as a set of constraints on the parameter values, thus complexifying the search process.

2.1.2 Approaches and Techniques

The first fuzzy modeling works were very similar to, and inspired by, the knowledge-engineering methods used in expert systems. They implemented

Zadeh's ideas by trying to build a fuzzy model directly from the expert knowledge in what we call the direct approach. The increasing availability of input-output data of the modeled processes, which is not specifically used to determine the structure or the parameters of the fuzzy model in the direct approach, together with the inherent difficulty to collect expert's knowledge, motivated the use of more automatic approaches to fuzzy modeling, in which only a part of the fuzzy model is built from *a priori* knowledge.

There exist a great number of fuzzy modeling methods differing in the search strategy they apply and in the amount of parameters they can search for—related directly with the part of the system they require to be pre-defined. Below, I briefly describe the direct approach to fuzzy modeling (Section 2.1.2.1) as well as other approaches based on classic identification algorithms (Section 2.1.2.2), on constructive learning methods (Section 2.1.2.3), and on bio-inspired techniques (Section 2.1.2.4).

2.1.2.1 The Direct Approach to Fuzzy Modeling. In this approach, the system is first linguistically described, based on the expert's *a priori* knowledge. It is then translated into the formal structure of a fuzzy model following the steps proposed by Zadeh [123]:

1. Selection of the input, state, and output variables (structural parameters);
2. Determination of the universes of discourse (structural parameters);
3. Determination of the linguistic labels into which these variables are partitioned (structural parameters);
4. Definition of the membership functions corresponding to each linguistic label (operational parameters);
5. Definition of the rules that describe the model's behavior (connective parameters);
6. Selection of an adequate reasoning mechanism (logic parameters);
7. Evaluation of the model adequacy.

Unfortunately, there is no general methodology for the implementation of the direct approach, which is more an art of intuition and experience than precise theory. This approach has been, however, successfully used since the first fuzzy system applications [53, 54] to present-day research [6, 21, 125].

One simple, and rather intuitive, improvement of the direct approach is the use of quantitative input-output information to update the membership-function values and/or the rule weights in order to fine-tune the knowledge contained in the fuzzy model [66].

2.1.2.2 Approaches Based on Classic Identification Algorithms. A fuzzy model is a special type of nonlinear model. In this context, fuzzy modeling may be done applying classic non-linear identification methods. These methods deals with an iterative, convergent, *estimation* of a set of numeric parameters, which are applied to a, usually pre-defined, model structure in order to approximate an expected behavior. In these fuzzy modeling approaches, the general structure of the fuzzy system (i.e., logic and structural parameters) is pre-defined, while the rest of the system (i.e., connective and operational parameters) is estimated.

The simplest methods apply linear least-squares parameter estimation as they assume that the parameters appear in a linear fashion into the model. Such linearity assumption limits their applicability in fuzzy modeling and asks for the development of methods applying nonlinear least-squares parameter estimation [51]. Recent works using this approach, apply identification methods such as orthogonal least-squares [104], gradient descent [15], quasi-Newton [97], Levenberg-Marquardt [16], or auto-regressive (AR) modeling [11].

2.1.2.3 Constructive Learning Approaches. In this approach, the *a priori* expert knowledge serves to direct the search process instead of being used to directly construct a part of, or the whole, fuzzy system. After an expert-guided definition of the logic parameters and of some of the structural parameters (mainly relevant variables and their universes of discourse), a sequence of learning algorithms is applied so as to progressively construct an adequate final fuzzy model. Most of the methods belonging to this class begin by identifying a large fuzzy system—even systems with one rule for each training case—satisfying certain performance criteria. They then apply a pruning strategy to reduce the size of the system while keeping an acceptable performance. Recent examples of this kind of approaches are presented by Espinosa and Vandewalle [18] and by Jin [42]. Other methods, as for example that of Rojas *et al.* [94], start with simple fuzzy systems and then iteratively increase the system's complexity, by adding new rules and membership functions, until a specified threshold of performance or of size is reached.

2.1.2.4 Bio-Inspired Approaches: Neuro-Fuzzy and Evolutionary-Fuzzy. As mentioned before, artificial neural networks, evolutionary algorithms, and fuzzy logic belong to the same family of bio-inspired methodologies. Indeed, they model in different extents natural processes such as evolution, learning, or reasoning. The dynamic and continuously growing research on these subjects, have allowed to identify the strengths and weaknesses of each methodology, motivating a relatively recent trend to combine them in order to take advantage of their complementarities. In fuzzy modeling, such combinations have originated hybrid techniques known as neuro-fuzzy systems and evolutionary fuzzy modeling. As these latter are presented in more detail in Section 2.2, I concentrate on the former.

Three main streams can be identified in the research on hybrid neural-fuzzy systems:

– Fuzzy-rule extraction from neural networks. This approach attempts to extract, in the form of fuzzy rules, the knowledge embedded in trained neural networks [14, 62, 102]. The main drawback of these techniques is that the access to the knowledge requires a previous rule-extraction phase.
– Neuro-fuzzy systems. These are fuzzy inference systems implemented as neural networks, taking advantage of their structural similarity (see Section 1.2.4). The main advantage of this kind of representation is that such hybrid systems can be optimized *via* powerful, well-known neural-network learning algorithms. ANFIS [40] is a well known neuro-fuzzy system consisting of a six-layer generalized network with supervised learning. Most of the current research on this area

is derived from the original neuro-fuzzy concept, either in new flavors (i.e., by changing the network structure or the learning strategy) [10, 70, 111], or in adaptation of existing methods to face new hard problems [52]. The main drawback of this approach is that the methods are intended to maximize accuracy, neglecting human interpretability. In many applications this is not acceptable.

– Interpretability-oriented neuro-fuzzy systems. A recent family of neuro-fuzzy systems are constructed respecting certain interpretability-related constraints (see Section 2.3) to keep permanent readability of the system during the learning process. One of the first steps towards interpretable neuro-fuzzy systems is represented by the suite of methods NEFCON, NEFCLASS, and NEFPROX [64, 65], based on a three-layer neuro-fuzzy architecture whose synaptic weights are constrained to respect the integrity of the fuzzy linguistic variables.

2.2 Evolutionary Fuzzy Modeling

Evolutionary algorithms are used to search large, and often complex, search spaces. They have proven worthwhile on numerous diverse problems, able to find near-optimal solutions given an adequate performance (fitness) measure. Fuzzy modeling can be considered as an optimization process where part or all of the parameters of a fuzzy system constitute the search space. Works investigating the application of evolutionary techniques in the domain of fuzzy modeling first appeared more than a decade ago [46, 47]. These focused mainly on the tuning of fuzzy inference systems involved in control tasks (e.g., cart-pole balancing, liquid-level system, and spacecraft rendezvous operation). Evolutionary fuzzy modeling has since been applied to an ever-growing number of domains, branching into areas as diverse as chemistry, medicine, telecommunications, biology, and geophysics. Alander [1] and Cordón and Herrera [12] presented detailed bibliographies on evolutionary fuzzy modeling up to 1996.

2.2.1 Applying Evolution to Fuzzy Modeling

Depending on several criteria—including the available *a priori* knowledge about the system, the size of the parameter set, and the availability and completeness of input-output data—artificial evolution can be applied in different stages of the fuzzy-parameter search. Three of the four categories of fuzzy parameters in Table 2.1 can be used to define targets for evolutionary fuzzy modeling: structural, connective, and operational parameters. As noted before, logical parameters are usually predefined by the designer based on experience. The aforementioned categories lead to the definition of three levels of fuzzy modeling: knowledge tuning, behavior learning, and structure learning, respectively. They are delineated below:

– **Knowledge tuning (operational parameters).** The evolutionary algorithm is used to tune the knowledge contained in the fuzzy system by finding membership-function values. An initial fuzzy system is defined by an expert. Then, the membership-function values are encoded in a genome, and an evolutionary algorithm is used to find systems with high performance. Evolution often overcomes the local-minima problem present in gradient descent-based methods. One of the major shortcomings of knowledge tuning is its dependency on the initial setting of the knowledge base.

– **Behavior learning (connective parameters).** In this approach, the membership functions are defined using expert knowledge or an identification technique (e.g. fuzzy clustering) is sufficient in order to define the membership functions; this determines, in fact, the maximum number of rules [120]. The evolutionary algorithm is used to find either the rule consequents, or an adequate subset of rules to be included in the rule base.

In the first case, the genome encodes directly the rule consequents. By not assigning consequents from the output set and creating a selection pressure by means of a carefully designed fitness function, one may obtain smaller rule bases. A faster approach encodes within the genome only a fixed set of user-defined rule templates. Selection of the specific rules is made by indexing them or by fully defining the antecedents and the consequents of each rule.

As the membership functions are fixed and predefined, this approach lacks the flexibility to modify substantially the system behavior. Furthermore, as the number of variables and membership functions increases, the curse of dimensionality becomes more pronounced and the interpretability of the system decreases rapidly.

– **Structure learning (structural parameters).** In many cases, the available information about the system is composed almost exclusively of input-output data, and specific knowledge about the system structure is scant. In such a case, evolution has to deal with the simultaneous design of rules, membership functions, and structural parameters. Some methods use a fixed-length genome encoding a fixed number of fuzzy rules along with the membership-function values. In this case the designer defines structural constraints according to the available knowledge of the problem characteristics. Other methods use variable-length genomes to allow evolution to discover the optimal size of the rule base. The strong interdependency among the parameters involved in this form of learning may slow down, or even prevent altogether, the convergence of the genetic algorithm.

2.2.2 Three Approaches to Behavior and Structure Learning

Both behavior and structure learning can be viewed as rule-base learning processes with different levels of complexity. They can thus be assimilated within other methods from machine learning, taking advantage of experience gained in this latter domain. In the evolutionary-algorithm community there are two major approaches for evolving such rule systems: the Michigan and the Pittsburgh approaches [60]. A more recent method has been proposed specifically for fuzzy modeling: the iterative rule learning approach [30]. These three approaches are outlined below.

- **The Michigan approach.** Each individual represents a *single* rule. The fuzzy inference system is represented by the *entire population*. Since several rules participate in the inference process, the rules are in constant competition for the best action to be proposed, and cooperate to form an efficient fuzzy system. The cooperative-competitive nature of this approach renders difficult the decision of which rules are ultimately responsible for good system behavior. It necessitates an effective credit-assignment policy to ascribe fitness values to individual rules.
- **The Pittsburgh approach.** The evolutionary algorithm maintains a population of candidate fuzzy systems, each individual representing an entire fuzzy system. Selection and genetic operators are used to produce new generations of fuzzy systems. Since evaluation is applied to the entire system, the credit-assignment problem is eschewed. This approach facilitates to include additional optimization criteria in the fitness function, thus affording the implementation of multi-objective optimization. The main shortcoming of this approach is its computational cost, since a population of full-fledged fuzzy systems has to be evaluated each generation.
- **The iterative rule learning approach.** As in the Michigan approach, each individual encodes a single rule. An evolutionary algorithm is used to find a single rule, thus providing a partial solution. The evolutionary algorithm is then used iteratively for the discovery of new rules, until an appropriate rule base is built. To prevent the process from finding redundant rules (i.e., rules covering the same input subspace), a penalization scheme is applied each time a new rule is added. This approach combines the speed of the Michigan approach with the simplicity of fitness evaluation of the Pittsburgh approach. However, as with other incremental rule-base construction methods, it can lead to a non-optimal partitioning of the antecedent space.

2.3 Interpretability Considerations

As mentioned before, the fuzzy-modeling process has to deal with an important trade-off between the *accuracy* and the *interpretability* of the model. The model is expected to provide high numeric precision while incurring as little a loss of linguistic descriptive power as possible. Currently, there exist no well-established definitions for interpretability of fuzzy systems, mainly due to the subjective nature of such a concept. However, some works have attempted to define objective criteria that facilitate the automatic modeling of interpretable fuzzy systems [29, 112].

The fuzzy system of Figure 1.11 processes information in three stages: the input interface (fuzzifier), the processing stage (inference engine), and the output interface (defuzzifier). The interface deals with linguistic variables and their corresponding labels. These linguistic variables define the *semantics* of the system. The inference process is performed using fuzzy rules that define the connection between input and output fuzzy variables. These fuzzy rules define the *syntax* of the fuzzy system. Fuzzy modelers must thus take into account both semantic and syntactic criteria to obtain interpretable systems. Below, I present some criteria that represent conditions driving fuzzy modeling toward human-interpretable systems together with strategies to satisfy them.

2.3.1 Semantic Criteria

The notion of linguistic variable formally requires associating a meaning to each fuzzy label [124]. Hence, each membership function should represent a linguistic term with a clear semantic meaning. For example, in Figure 2.1, the fuzzy variable *Triglycerides* has three meaningful labels: **Normal**, **High**, and **Very High**. The following semantic criteria describe a set of properties that the membership functions of a fuzzy variable should possess in order to facilitate the task of assigning linguistic terms [75, 77, 82]. The focus is on the meaning of the ensemble of labels instead of the absolute meaning of each term in isolation.

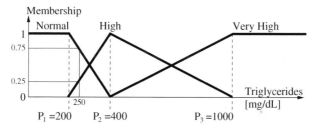

Fig. 2.1. Semantically correct fuzzy variable: *Triglycerides* has three possible fuzzy values, labeled **Normal**, **High**, and **Very High**, plotted above as degree of membership versus input value. The values P_i, setting the trapezoid and triangle apices, define the membership functions. In the figure, an example input value 250 mg/dl is assigned the membership values $\mu_{Normal}(250) = 0.75$, $\mu_{High}(250) = 0.25$, and $\mu_{VeryHigh}(250) = 0$. Note that $\mu_{Normal}(250) + \mu_{High}(250) + \mu_{VeryHigh}(250) = 1$.

- *Distinguishability.* Each linguistic label should have semantic meaning and the fuzzy set should clearly define a range in the universe of discourse of the variable. In the example of Figure 2.1, to describe variable *Triglycerides* we used three meaningful labels: **Normal**, **High**, and **Very High**. Their membership functions are defined using parameters P_1, P_2, and P_3.
- *Justifiable number of elements.* The number of linguistic labels—i.e., the number of membership functions of a variable—should be compatible with the number of conceptual entities a human being can handle. This number, that should not exceed the limit of 7 ± 2 distinct terms, is related directly with the expertise of the human interacting with the system. In the example of Figure 2.1, while a patient would not feel comfortable with more than the three labels defined, a physician should certainly handle more labels.
- *Coverage.* Any element from the universe of discourse should belong to at least one of the fuzzy sets. That is, its membership value must be different than zero

for at least one of the linguistic labels. More generally, a minimum level of coverage may be defined, giving rise to the concept of *strong coverage*. Referring to Figure 2.1, we see that any value along the x-axis belongs to at least one fuzzy set; no value lies outside the range of all sets.

– *Normalization.* Since all labels have semantic meaning, then, for each label, at least one element of the universe of discourse should have a membership value equal to one. In Figure 2.1, we observe that all three sets **Normal**, **High**, and **Very High** have elements with membership value equal to 1.

– *Complementarity.* For each element of the universe of discourse, the sum of all its membership values should be equal to one (as in the example in Figure 2.1). This guarantees uniform distribution of meaning among the elements.

2.3.2 Syntactic Criteria

A fuzzy rule relates one or more input-variable conditions, called antecedents, to their corresponding output fuzzy conclusions, called consequents. The example rule presented in Figure 2.2, associates the conditions **High** and **Middle** of the input variables *Triglycerides* and *Age*, respectively, with the conclusion **Moderate** of the output variable *Cardiac risk*. The linguistic adequacy of a fuzzy rule base lies in the interpretability of each rule as well as in that of the whole set of rules. The following syntactic criteria define some conditions which—if satisfied by the rule base—reinforce the interpretability of a fuzzy system [29].

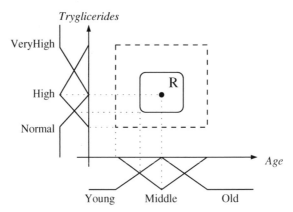

Fig. 2.2. Example of a fuzzy rule and its firing range. The rule **if** *Triglycerides* **is** *High* **and** *Age* **is** *Middle* **then** *Cardiac risk* **is** *Moderate*, marked as **R**, is (partially) fired by input values into the dashed-line rectangle (i.e. $\mu(R) > 0$). The solid-line rectangle denotes the region where $\mu(R) \geq 0.5$.

– *Completeness.* For any possible input vector, at least one rule should be fired to prevent the fuzzy system from getting blocked.

- *Rule-base simplicity.* The set of rules must be as small as possible. If, however, the rule base is still large, rendering hard a global understanding of the system, the number of rules that fire simultaneously for any input vector must remain low in order to furnish a simple local view of the behavior.
- *Single-rule readability.* The number of conditions implied in the antecedent of a rule should be compatible with the aforementioned number of conceptual entities a human being can handle (i.e., number of entities $\leq 7 \pm 2$).
- *Consistency.* If two or more rules are simultaneously fired, their consequents should not be contradictory, i.e., they should be semantically close.

2.3.3 Strategies to Satisfy Semantic and Syntactic Criteria

The criteria presented above, intended to assess interpretability of a fuzzy system, define a number of restrictions on the definition of fuzzy parameters. Semantic criteria limit the choice of membership functions, while syntactic criteria bind the fuzzy rule base. I present below some strategies to apply these restrictions when defining a fuzzy model.

- *Linguistic labels shared by all rules.* A number of fuzzy sets is defined for each variable, which are interpreted as linguistic labels and shared by all the rules [29]. In other words, each variable has a unique semantic definition. This results in a grid partition of the input space as illustrated in Figure 2.3. To satisfy the completeness criterion, we normally use a fully defined rule base, meaning that it contains all the possible rules, The example system shown in Figure 2.4a contains all nine possible rules of the form **if** *Triglycerides* **is** *label* **and** *Age* **is** *label* **then** *Cardiac risk* **is** .... Label sharing by itself facilitates but does not guarantee the semantic integrity of each variable. More conditions are necessary.

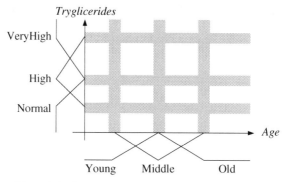

Fig. 2.3. Grid partition of the input space. In this example, two semantically correct input variables, each with three labels, divide the input space into a grid of nine regions.

- *Normal, orthogonal membership functions.* The membership functions of two successive labels must be complementary (i.e., their sum must be equal to one) in their overlapping region, whatever form they have [18, 112]. Moreover, in such regions each label must ascend from zero to unity membership values [75, 77]. The variables presented in Figures 2.1 and 2.3, satisfy these requirements.

- *Don't-care conditions.* A fully defined rule base, as that shown in Figure 2.4a, becomes impractical for high-dimension systems. The number of rules in a fully defined rule base exponentially increases as the number of input variables increases (e.g., a system with five variables, each with three labels, would contain $3^5 = 243$ rules). Moreover, given that each rule antecedent contains a condition for each variable, the rules might be too lengthy to be understandable, and too specific to describe general circumstances.

  To tackle these two problems some authors use *"don't-care"* as a valid input label [39, 75, 77]. Variables in a given rule that are marked with a *don't-care* label are considered as irrelevant. For example, in the rule base shown in Figure 2.4b two rules, R_A and R_B, containing *don't-care* labels cover almost half of the input space. The rule R_A:

  if *Triglycerides* **is** *don't-care* **and** *Age* **is** *Old* **then** *Cardiac risk* **is** *Moderate*,

  covers the space of three rules (i.e., R_3, R_6, and R_9 in Figure 2.4a) and is interpreted as:

  if *Age* **is** *Old* **then** *Cardiac risk* **is** *Moderate*.

  In the same way, the rule R_B is interpreted as:

  if *Triglycerides* **is** *VeryHigh* **then** *Cardiac risk* **is** ....

  Although *don't-care* labels allow a reduction of rule-base size, their main advantage is the improvement of rule readability.

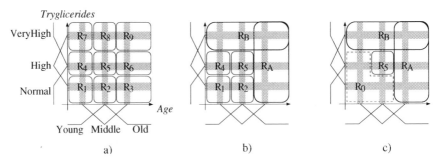

Fig. 2.4. Strategies to define a complete rule base. a) Fully defined rule base. b) *don't-care* labels. c) Default rule. By definition, the activation of the (fuzzy) default rule is $\mu(R_0) = 1 - max(\mu(R_i))$, with $i = \{1, 2, 3, \ldots\}$. The rectangles denote the region where $\mu(R_i) \geq 0.5$.

- *Default rule.* In many cases, the behavior of a system exhibits only a few regions of interest, which can be described by a small number of rules (e.g., R_5, R_A, and R_B in Figure 2.4b). To describe the rest of the input space, a simple default action, provided by the default rule, would be enough [114]. The example in Figure 2.4c shows that the default rule, named R_0, covers the space of rules R_1, R_2, and R_4. By definition, a default condition is true when all other rule conditions are

false. In a fuzzy context, the default rule is as true as all the others are false. Consequently, the activation degree of the default rule, $\mu(R_0)$, is thus given by $\mu(R_0) = 1 - max(\mu(R_i))$, where $\mu(R_i)$ is the activation degree of the i-th rule.
 - *Linguistic fitness.* Some linguistic criteria can be reinforced by taking them into account to compute the fitness value of a given fuzzy system. Size factors, related with simplicity and readability, such as the number of rules effectively used or the number of conditions implied in the rule antecedents can be easily quantified and included in the fitness function.

2.4 Example: Medical Diagnosis

A major class of problems in medical science involves the diagnosis of disease, based upon various tests performed upon the patient. When several tests are involved, the ultimate diagnosis may be difficult to obtain, even for a medical expert. This has given rise, over the past few decades, to computerized diagnostic tools, intended to aid the physician in making sense out of the welter of data.

A prime target for such computerized tools is in the domain of cancer diagnosis. Specifically, where breast cancer is concerned, the treating physician is interested in ascertaining whether the patient under examination exhibits the symptoms of a benign case, or whether her case is a malignant one.

A good computerized diagnostic tool should possess two characteristics, which are often in conflict. First, the tool must attain the highest possible performance, i.e., diagnose the presented cases correctly as being either *benign* or *malignant*. Second, it would be highly beneficial for such a diagnostic system to be interpretable. This means that the physician is not faced with a black box that simply spouts answers (albeit correct) with no explanation; rather, we would like for the system to provide some insight as to how it derives its outputs.

Thanks to their linguistic representation and their numeric behavior, fuzzy systems can provide both characteristics. Moreover, an evolutionary fuzzy modeling approach, carefully setup following the strategies presented in Section 2.3.3, can deal with the trade-off between performance and interpretability. Following, I describe the Wisconsin breast cancer diagnosis (WBCD) problem. Section 2.4.2 then describes a genetic-fuzzy approach to the WBCD problem, while Section 2.4.3 delineates the results. In Section 2.4.4, I discuss the issue of obtaining a confidence measure of the system's output, going beyond a mere binary, benign-malignant classification. Finally, Section 2.4.5, briefly describes two further experiments that I carried out.

2.4.1 The Wisconsin Breast Cancer Diagnosis (WBCD) Problem

This section presents the medical-diagnosis problem which is the object of my study, and the fuzzy system I propose to solve it.

Breast cancer is the most common cancer among women, excluding skin cancer. The presence of a breast mass[1] is an alert sign, but it does not always indicate a malignant cancer. Fine needle aspiration (FNA)[2] of breast masses is a cost-effective, non-traumatic, and mostly non-invasive diagnostic test that obtains information needed to evaluate malignancy.

The WBCD database [58] is the result of the efforts made at the University of Wisconsin Hospital for accurately diagnosing breast masses based solely on an FNA test [55]. Nine visually assessed characteristics of an FNA sample considered relevant for diagnosis were identified, and assigned an integer value between 1 and 10. The measured variables are as follows:

1 Clump thickness (v_1);
2 uniformity of cell size (v_2);
3 uniformity of cell shape (v_3);
4 marginal adhesion (v_4);
5 single epithelial cell size (v_5);
6 bare nuclei (v_6);
7 bland chromatin (v_7);
8 normal nucleoli (v_8);
9 mitosis (v_9).

The diagnostics in the WBCD database were furnished by specialists in the field. The database itself consists of 683 cases, with each entry representing the classification for a certain ensemble of measured values:

$case$	v_1	v_2	v_3	$\cdots$	v_9	$diagnostic$
1	5	1	1	$\cdots$	1	$benign$
2	5	4	4	$\cdots$	1	$benign$
$\vdots$	$\vdots$	$\vdots$	$\vdots$	$\ddots$	$\vdots$	$\vdots$
683	4	8	8	$\cdots$	1	$malignant$

Note that the diagnostics do not provide any information about the degree of benignity or malignancy.

There are several studies based on this database. Bennet and Mangasarian [4] used linear programming techniques, obtaining a 99.6% classification rate on 487 cases (the reduced database available at the time). However, their solution exhibits little understandability, i.e., diagnostic decisions are essentially black boxes, with no explanation as to how they were attained. With increased interpretability in mind as a prior objective, a number of researchers have applied the method of extracting Boolean rules from neural networks [101–103, 107]. Their results are encouraging, exhibiting both good performance and a reduced number of rules and relevant input variables. Nevertheless, these systems use Boolean rules and are not capable of furnishing the user with a measure of confidence for the decision made. My own

---

[1] Most breast cancers are detected as a lump or mass on the breast, by self-examination, by mammography, or by both [56].

[2] Fine needle aspiration is an outpatient procedure that involves using a small-gauge needle to extract fluid directly from a breast mass [56].

work on the evolution of fuzzy rules for the WBCD problem has shown that it is possible to obtain diagnostic systems exhibiting high performance, coupled with interpretability and a confidence measure [?, 73–75].

2.4.2 A Genetic-Fuzzy Approach to the WBCD Problem

The solution scheme I propose for the WBCD problem is depicted in Figure 2.5. It consists of a fuzzy system and a threshold unit. The fuzzy system computes a continuous appraisal value of the malignancy of a case, based on the input values. The threshold unit then outputs a *benign* or *malignant* diagnostic according to the fuzzy system's output.

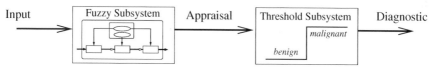

Fig. 2.5. Proposed diagnosis system. Note that the fuzzy subsystem displayed to the left is in fact the entire fuzzy inference system of Figure 1.11.

In order to evolve the fuzzy model we must make some preliminary decisions about the fuzzy system itself and about the genetic algorithm encoding.

2.4.2.1 Fuzzy System Parameters. My previous knowledge about the WBCD problem represents valuable information to be used for my choice of fuzzy parameters (Table 2.1). When defining the setup, I took into consideration the following three results concerning the composition of potential high-performance systems: (1) small number of rules; (2) small number of variables; and (3) monotonicity of the input variables. Some fuzzy models forgo interpretability in the interest of improved performance. Where medical diagnosis is concerned, interpretability is the major advantage of fuzzy systems. This motivates to take into account the interpretability criteria presented in Section 2.3 to define constraints on the fuzzy parameters. Referring to Table 2.1, I delineate below the fuzzy-system setup:

- *Logical parameters:* singleton-type fuzzy systems; min-max fuzzy operators; orthogonal, trapezoidal input membership functions (see Figure 2.6); weighted-average defuzzification.
- *Structural parameters:* two input membership functions (*Low* and *High*; see Figure 2.6); two output singletons (*benign* and *malignant*); a user-configurable number of rules. The relevant variables are one of the evolutionary objectives.
- *Connective parameters:* the antecedents of the rules are searched by the evolutionary algorithm. The consequents of the rules are predefined, the algorithm finds rules for the *benign* diagnostic, while the default-rule consequent is the *malignant* diagnostic. All rules have unitary weight.

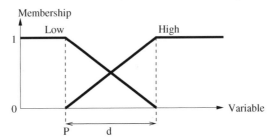

Fig. 2.6. Input fuzzy variables for the WBCD problem. Each fuzzy variable has two possible fuzzy values labeled **Low** and **High**, and orthogonal membership functions, plotted above as degree of membership versus input value. P and d define the start point and the length of membership function edges, respectively.

– *Operational parameters:* the input membership-function values are to be found by the evolutionary algorithm. For the output singletons I used the values 2 and 4, for *benign* and *malignant*, respectively.

2.4.2.2 The Evolutionary Setup. The problem, at this stage, consists of searching for three fuzzy-system parameters: input membership functions, antecedents of rules, and relevant variables. I applied a Pittsburgh-like approach, using a simple genetic algorithm [113] to search for individuals whose genomes, encoding these three parameters, are defined as follows:

– Membership-function parameters. There are nine variables ($v_1 - v_9$), each with two parameters P and d, defining the start point and the length of the membership-function edges, respectively (Figure 2.6).
– Antecedents. The i-th rule has the form:
  if (v_1 **is** A_1^i) **and ... and** (v_9 **is** A_9^i) **then** (*output* **is** *benign*),
  where A_j^i represents the membership function applicable to variable v_j. A_j^i can take on the values: 1 (*Low*), 2 (*High*), or 0 or 3 (*Don't Care*).
– Relevant variables are searched for implicitly by letting the algorithm choose *Don't care* labels as valid antecedents; in such a case the respective variable is considered irrelevant (See Section 2.3.3).

Table 2.2 delineates the parameter encoding and Figure 2.7 shows a sample genome encoding a whole fuzzy system.

Table 2.2. Parameter encoding of an individual's genome. Total genome length is $54 + 18N_r$, where N_r denotes the number of rules (N_r is set *a priori* to a value between 1–5, and is fixed during the genetic-algorithm run).

Parameter	Values	Bits	Qty	Total bits
P	$\{1,2,\ldots,8\}$	3	9	27
d	$\{1,2,\ldots,8\}$	3	9	27
A	$\{0,1,2,3\}$	2	$9 \times N_r$	$18 \times N_r$

P_1	d_1	P_2	d_2	P_3	d_3	P_4	d_4	P_5	d_5	
4	3	1	5	2	7	1	1	1	6	...

P_6	d_6	P_7	d_7	P_8	d_8	P_9	d_9	
3	7	4	6	7	1	1	5	...

A_1^1	A_2^1	A_3^1	A_4^1	A_5^1	A_6^1	A_7^1	A_8^1	A_9^1
0	1	3	3	2	3	1	3	1

(a)

Database

	v_1	v_2	v_3	v_4	v_5	v_6	v_7	v_8	v_9
P	4	1	2	1	1	3	4	7	1
d	3	5	7	1	6	7	6	1	5

Rule base

Rule 1	**if** (v_2 **is** *Low*) **and** (v_5 **is** *High*) **and** (v_7 **is** *Low*) **and** (v_9 **is** *Low*) **then** (*output* **is** *benign*)
Default	**else** (*output* **is** *malignant*)

(b)

Fig. 2.7. Example of a genome for a single-rule system. (a) Genome encoding. The first 18 positions encode the parameters P and d for the nine variables v_1–v_9. The rest encode the membership function applicable for the nine antecedents of each rule. (b) Interpretation. Database and rule base of the single-rule system encoded by (a). The parameters P and d are interpreted as illustrated in Figure 2.6.

To evolve the fuzzy inference system, I used a genetic algorithm with a fixed population size of 200 individuals, and fitness-proportionate selection (Section 1.3). The algorithm terminates when the maximum number of generations, G_{max}, is reached (I set $G_{max} = 2000 + 500 \times N_r$, i.e., dependent on the number of rules used in the run), or when the increase in fitness of the best individual over five successive generations falls below a certain threshold (in these experiments, I used threshold values between 2×10^{-7} and 4×10^{-6}).

My fitness function combines three criteria: (1) F_c: classification performance, computed as the percentage of cases correctly classified; (2) F_e: the quadratic difference between the continuous appraisal value (in the range $[2, 4]$) and the correct discrete diagnosis given by the WBCD database (either 2 or 4); and (3) F_v: the average number of variables per active rule. The fitness function is given by $F = F_c - \alpha F_v - \beta F_e$, where $\alpha = 0.05$ and $\beta = 0.01$ (these latter values were derived empirically). F_c, the ratio of correctly diagnosed cases, is the most important measure of performance. F_v measures the interpretability, penalizing systems with a large number of variables per rule (on average). F_e adds selection pressure towards systems with low quadratic error.

2.4.3 Results

The evolutionary experiments performed fall into three categories, in accordance with the data repartitioning into two distinct sets: training and test (or evaluation). The three experimental categories are: (1) the training set contains all 683 cases

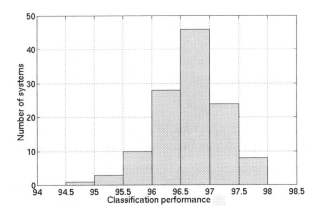

Fig. 2.8. Summary of results of 120 evolutionary runs. The histogram depicts the number of systems exhibiting a given performance level at the end of the evolutionary run. The performance considered is that of the best individual of the run, measured as the overall percentage of correctly classified cases over the entire database.

of the WBCD database, while the test set is empty; (2) the training set contains 75% of the WBCD cases, and the test set contains the remaining 25% of the cases; (3) the training set contains 50% of the WBCD cases, and the test set contains the remaining 50% of the cases. In the last two categories, the choice of training-set cases is done randomly, and is performed anew at the outset of every evolutionary run. The number of rules per system was also fixed at the outset, to be between one and five, i.e., evolution seeks a system with an *a priori* given number of rules (the choice of number of rules per system determines the final structure of the genome, as presented in Table 2.2).

A total of 120 evolutionary runs were performed, all of which found systems whose classification performance exceeds 94.5%. In particular, considering the best individual per run (i.e., the evolved system with the highest classification success rate), 78 runs led to a fuzzy system whose performance exceeds 96.5%, and of these, 8 runs found systems whose performance exceeds 97.5%; these results are summarized in Figure 2.8. Table 2.3 presents the average performance obtained by the genetic algorithm over all 120 evolutionary runs, divided according to the three experimental categories discussed above. A more detailed account of these results is presented in Table 2.4.5 at the end of this chapter, which lists the top evolved 45 systems. Note that the results using a data distribution of 75% of cases for training and 25% for test suggest good generalization capabilities of the method. Indeed, the best 2, 3, and 4-rule systems of this category perform slightly better on the test set than on the training set. A more detailed generalization analysis goes beyond the scope of this preliminary example.

Table 2.4 shows the results of the best systems obtained with the fuzzy-genetic approach. The number of rules per system was fixed at the outset to be between one

Table 2.3. Summary of results of 120 evolutionary runs, divided according to the three experimental categories discussed in the text (i.e., the three classes which differ in the training-set to test-set ratio). The table lists the average performance over all 120 runs, where the averaging is done over the best individual of each run. The performance value denotes the percentage of cases correctly classified. Three such performance values are shown: (1) performance over the training set; (2) performance over the test set; and (3) overall performance, considering the entire database. In addition, the average number of variables per rule is also shown.

Training/test ratio	Performance			Variables per rule
	Training set	Test set	Overall	
100% / 0%	–	–	96.97%	3.32
75% / 25%	97.00%	96.02%	96.76%	3.46
50% / 50%	97.71%	94.73%	96.23%	3.41

and five, i.e., evolution seeks a system with an *a priori* given number of rules. A comparison of these systems with other approaches is presented in Section 4.1.2.

Table 2.4. Results of the best systems evolved by the fuzzy-genetic approach. Shown below are the classification performance values of the top systems obtained by these approaches, along with the average number of variables-per-rule. Results are divided into five classes, in accordance with the number of rules-per-system, going from one-rule systems to five-rule ones.

Rules-per-system	Performance	variables-per-rule
1	97.07%	4
2	97.36%	3
3	97.80%	4.7
4	97.80%	4.8
5	97.51%	3.4

I next describe three of my top-performance systems, which serve to exemplify the solutions found by my evolutionary approach. The first system, delineated in Figure 2.9, consists of three rules (note that the default rule is not counted as an active rule). Taking into account all three criteria of performance—classification rate, number of rules per system, and average number of variables per rule— this system can be considered the top one over all 120 evolutionary runs. It obtains 98.2% correct classification rate over the benign cases, 97.07% correct classification rate over the malignant cases,[3] and an overall classification rate (i.e., over the entire database) of 97.8%.

A thorough test of this three-rule system revealed that the second rule (Figure 2.9) is never actually used, i.e., is fired by none of the input cases. Thus, it can be eliminated altogether from the rule base, resulting in a two-rule system (also reducing the average number of variables per rule from 4.7 to 4).

Database

	v_1	v_2	v_3	v_4	v_5	v_6	v_7	v_8	v_9
P	3	5	2	2	8	1	4	5	4
d	5	2	1	2	4	7	3	5	2

Rule base

Rule 1   **if** (v_3 **is** *Low*) **and** (v_7 **is** *Low*) **and** (v_8 **is** *Low*) **and** (v_9 **is** *Low*) **then** (*output* **is** *benign*)

Rule 2   **if** (v_1 **is** *Low*) **and** (v_2 **is** *Low*) **and** (v_3 **is** *High*) **and** (v_4 **is** *Low*) **and** (v_5 **is** *High*) **and** (v_9 **is** *Low*) **then** (*output* **is** *benign*)

Rule 3   **if** (v_1 **is** *Low*) **and** (v_4 **is** *Low*) **and** (v_6 **is** *Low*) **and** (v_8 **is** *Low*) **then** (*output* **is** *benign*)

Default   **else** (*output* **is** *malignant*)

Fig. 2.9. The best evolved, fuzzy diagnostic system with three rules. It exhibits an overall classification rate of 97.8%, and an average of 4.7 variables per rule.

Can the genetic algorithm automatically discover a two-rule system, i.e., without recourse to any post-processing (such as that described in the previous paragraph)? My results have shown that this is indeed the case—one such solution is presented in Figure 2.10. It obtains 97.3% correct classification rate over the benign cases, 97.49% correct classification rate over the malignant cases, and an overall classification rate of 97.36%.

Database

	v_1	v_2	v_3	v_4	v_5	v_6	v_7	v_8	v_9
P	1	1	1		6	2		3	
d	5	3	2		7	4		1	

Rule base

Rule 1   **if** (v_1 **is** *Low*) **and** (v_3 **is** *Low*) **then** (*output* **is** *benign*)

Rule 2   **if** (v_2 **is** *Low*) **and** (v_5 **is** *Low*) **and** (v_6 **is** *Low*) **and** (v_8 **is** *Low*) **then** (*output* **is** *benign*)

Default   **else** (*output* **is** *malignant*)

Fig. 2.10. The best evolved, fuzzy diagnostic system with two rules. It exhibits an overall classification rate of 97.36%, and an average of 3 variables per rule.

2.4.4 Diagnostic Confidence

So far, we have been using the evolved fuzzy systems to ultimately produce a binary classification value—*benign* or *malignant*—with no finer gradations. Going back to Figure 2.5, we note that the diagnostic system comprises in fact two subsystems: the first subsystem consists of the (evolved) fuzzy system, which, upon presentation of an input (in this case, a WBCD database entry) proceeds to produce a *continuous* appraisal value; this value is then passed along to the second subsystem—the threshold unit—which produces the final binary output (*benign* or *malignant*). The first subsystem (the fuzzy system) is the one evolved in this approach. The threshold subsystem simply outputs *malignant* if the appraisal value is below a fixed threshold value, and outputs *benign* otherwise. The threshold value is assigned by the user through knowledge of the problem at hand.

To gain an intuitive understanding of how a classification value is computed, let me sketch a simple example. Referring to the system of Figure 2.5, assume that the following values are presented as inputs:

	v_1	v_2	v_3	v_4	v_5	v_6	v_7	v_8	v_9
Value	4	3	1	1	2	1	4	8	1

The membership value of each variable is then computed in accordance with the (evolved) database of Figure 2.9:

	v_1	v_2	v_3	v_4	v_5	v_6	v_7	v_8	v_9
μ_{Low}	0.8	1	1	1	1	1	1	0.4	1
μ_{High}	0.2	0	0	0	0	0	0	0.6	0

This completes the fuzzification phase. Having computed these membership values, the inference engine can now go on to compute the so-called truth value of each rule. This truth value is computed by applying the fuzzy AND operator (Section 1.2) to combine the antecedent clauses (the membership values) in a fuzzy manner; this results in the output truth value, namely, a continuous value which represents the rule's degree of activation. Thus, a rule is not merely either activated or not, but in fact is activated to a certain degree—represented by a value between 0 and 1. In this example, the rule activation values are as follows (remember that we "chucked out" rule 2, since it was found to never fire):

	Rule 1	Rule 3	Default
Truth value	0.4	0.4	0.6

The inference engine (Figure 1.11) now goes on to apply the aggregation operator (Section 1.2), combining the continuous rule activation values to produce a fuzzy output with a certain truth value. The defuzzifier then kicks in (Figure 1.11), producing the final continuous value of the fuzzy inference system; this latter value is the appraisal value that is passed on to the threshold unit (Figure 2.5). In this example the appraisal value is 2.86.

In general, the appraisal value computed by my evolved fuzzy systems is in the range [2, 4]. I chose to place the threshold value at 3, with inferior values classified as benign, and superior values classified as malignant . Thus, in this example, the appraisal value of 2.86 is classified as benign—which is correct.

This case in the WBCD database produces an appraisal value (2.86) which is among the closest to the threshold value. Most other cases result in an appraisal value that lies close to one of the extremes (i.e., close to either 2 or 4). Thus, in a sense, we can say that we are somewhat less confident where this case is concerned, with respect to most other entries in the WBCD database; specifically, the appraisal value can accompany the final output of the diagnostic system, serving as a confidence measure. This demonstrates a prime advantage of fuzzy systems, namely, the ability to output not only a (binary) classification, but also a measure representing the system's confidence in its output.

Table 2.5. Results of evolutionary runs in which the variables-per-rule constraint has been removed. Results are divided into five classes going from three-rule systems to seven-rule ones. I performed 5–7 runs per class, totaling 31 runs in all; shown below are the resulting best systems as well as the average per class. Results include the overall classification performance and the average number of variables-per-rule in parentheses.

Rules-per-system	Best system	Average
3	97.66% (5.3)	97.49% (5.4)
4	98.24% (5.8)	97.63% (5.4)
5	97.95% (6)	97.63% (5.6)
6	98.10% (6.2)	97.77% (5.4)
7	97.95% (5)	97.88% (5.2)
Total	98.24% (5.8)	97.68% (5.4)

2.4.5 Further Experiments

In this section I describe two further experiments carried out; these are aimed at searching for systems with yet better performance than obtained hitherto—though possibly at the expense of some other aspect of the resulting system.

As noted in Section 2.1, fuzzy systems offer a major advantage in terms of (possible) linguistic integrity, i.e., interpretability by humans. With this goal in mind, the experiments described previously were constrained: I limited both the number of rules per system, as well as the number of variables per rule (See Section 2.3). This latter constraint was incorporated by favoring systems with few variables-per-rule via the F_v coefficient: lower F_v, meaning fewer variables-per-rule, entails higher overall fitness.

Can higher-performance systems be obtained by eliminating the F_v factor (albeit at the cost of reduced interpretability due to more complicated rules)? This was the aim of the first of the two experiments described herein. I eliminated, besides the F_v measure, the F_e factor, the resulting fitness function thus containing solely F_c. My intent was to provide selection pressure for but one goal: overall classification performance. With this aim in mind I was also more "generous" with the number of rules per system: whereas previously this was set to a (fixed) value between one and five, herein I set this value to be between three and seven.

I performed a total of 31 evolutionary runs, the results of which are summarized in Table 2.5. Note that my previously best system (Figure 2.9) obtained 97.8% overall classification performance, while Table 2.5 shows an evolved system with a 98.24% classification rate. This latter system is thus able to correctly classify 3 additional cases. This small improvement in performance carries, however, a price: the slightly better system comprises four rules with an average of 5.8 variables per rule, whereas the previous one (Figure 2.9) contains but three rules with an average of 4.7 variables per rule; I have thus traded off interpretability for performance. It is noteworthy that this choice can be easily implemented in this approach.

As explained in Section 2.4.2, the active rules diagnose benignity, with the default diagnosis being malignancy; this means that the `if` conditions have *benign* as a consequent, whereas the `else` condition has *malignant* as a consequent. The second experiment sought to find out what would happen if this were reversed, i.e., could better systems be evolved with benignity as the default diagnosis? Table 2.6 delineates the results of 27 evolutionary runs. While I did not improve upon the results of the malignancy-default systems of Section 2.4.3, I did note a tendency toward a smaller number of variables-per-rule. The highest-performance system found in this experiment is fully specified in Figure 2.11. It comprises five rules with an average of 2.8 variables-per-rule, exhibiting the same overall performance (97.8%) as the three-rule, 4.7 average-variables-per-rule system of Figure 2.9. This nicely illustrates the tradeoff between these two parameters: number of rules per system and average number of variables per rule.

Table 2.6. Results of evolutionary runs in which the default diagnosis is *benign* (rather than *malignant*). Results are divided into five classes going from one-rule systems to five-rule ones. I performed 4–6 runs per class, totaling 27 runs in all; shown below are the resulting best systems as well as the average per class. Results include the overall classification performance and the average number of variables-per-rule in parentheses.

Rules-per-system	Best system	Average
1	94.73% (2)	94.44% (2)
2	96.93% (1.5)	96.34% (1.8)
3	97.36% (2)	96.57% (1.7)
4	97.07% (1.8)	97.00% (2)
5	97.80% (2.8)	96.52% (2.2)
Total	97.80% (2.8)	97.68% (1.9)

Database

	v_1	v_2	v_3	v_4	v_5	v_6	v_7	v_8	v_9
P	4	2	2	8	4	2	2	5	6
d	8	5	5	1	8	6	3	4	5

Rule base

Rule 1	**if** (v_2 **is** *High*) **and** (v_7 **is** *High*) **then** (*output* **is** *malignant*)
Rule 2	**if** (v_2 **is** *High*) **and** (v_3 **is** *High*) **and** (v_4 **is** *Low*) **and** (v_8 **is** *High*) **and** (v_9 **is** *Low*) **then** (*output* **is** *malignant*)
Rule 3	**if** (v_3 **is** *High*) **and** (v_6 **is** *High*) **then** (*output* **is** *malignant*)
Rule 4	**if** (v_3 **is** *Low*) **and** (v_5 **is** *High*) **and** (v_8 **is** *High*) **then** (*output* **is** *malignant*)
Rule 5	**if** (v_1 **is** *High*) **and** (v_6 **is** *High*) **then** (*output* **is** *malignant*)
Default	**else** (*output* **is** *benign*)

Fig. 2.11. The best evolved, fuzzy diagnostic system with *malignant* active rules. It exhibits an overall classification rate of 97.80%, and in average 2.8 variables per rule.

Table 2.7. Summary of top 45 evolutionary runs (of 120) described in Section 2.4.3, divided according to the three experimental categories discussed in the text (i.e., the three classes which differ in the training-set to test-set ratio). For each of the 45 evolved systems, the table lists its fitness value, its performance, and its average number of variables-per-rule. As explained in Section 2.4.3, the performance value denotes the percentage of cases correctly classified. Three such performance values are shown: (1) performance over the training set; (2) performance over the test set; and (3) overall performance, considering the entire database.

Rules	100% / 0%			75% / 25%					50% / 50%				
	fitness	performance	variables	fitness	training	test	performance	variables	fitness	training	test	performance	variables
1	0.9548	96.78	3	0.9553	97.46	95.91	97.07	4	0.9637	97.66	95.6	96.63	3
	0.9548	96.78	3	0.9597	97.27	95.32	96.78	3	0.9607	97.37	95.01	96.19	3
	0.9533	96.63	3	0.9557	96.88	96.49	96.78	3	0.9607	97.37	95.01	96.19	3
2	0.9576	97.36	3.5	0.9598	97.27	97.66	97.36	3	0.9603	97.95	95.89	96.93	4
	0.9593	97.22	3	0.9548	97.07	96.49	96.93	3.5	0.9579	97.08	96.77	96.93	3
	0.9578	97.07	3	0.9648	97.46	94.74	96.78	2.5	0.9636	97.95	94.43	96.19	3.5
3	0.9548	97.8	4.67	0.9577	97.27	97.66	97.36	3.33	0.9659	97.66	95.89	96.78	2.67
	0.9554	97.66	4.33	0.9557	97.27	97.08	97.22	3.67	0.9546	97.37	95.89	96.63	4
	0.9594	97.22	3	0.9577	97.27	95.91	96.93	3.33	0.9626	97.95	95.01	96.49	3.67
4	0.9543	97.8	4.75	0.952	97.27	98.25	97.51	4.25	0.9755	99.12	95.6	97.36	3.5
	0.9529	97.51	4.5	0.9563	97.07	96.49	96.93	3.25	0.971	98	95.89	97.36	3.75
	0.9594	97.22	3	0.9591	97.66	94.15	96.78	3.75	0.965	98.25	95.31	96.78	3.75
5	0.9599	97.51	3.4	0.9587	97.66	97.08	97.51	3.8	0.9586	97.66	96.77	97.22	3.8
	0.9483	97.36	5	0.9575	97.66	97.08	97.51	4	0.9756	98.83	94.72	96.78	3
	0.9584	97.36	3.4	0.9561	97.27	96.49	97.07	3.6	0.9623	98.25	95.01	96.63	4.2

3 Coevolutionary Fuzzy Modeling

In the simplified models of evolution discussed in Section 1.3, we consider individuals belonging to a single species—i.e., sharing the same genetic encoding, and reproducing with each other. We assume this species evolves in isolation, in an almost unchanging environment. In nature, species live in the niches afforded by other species, modifying themselves and the environment and being affected by such modifications.

Over time, the evolution of many species has been influenced by interactions with other species. Species that have mutually influenced one another's evolution are said to have *coevolved* [90]. Flowers coevolved with the insects that pollinated them and fed on their nectar in a mutualist relationship where reproductive success (fitness) of one species is beneficial for other species' survival. On the other hand, predator-prey interaction constitutes an example of competitive coevolution where the survival of individuals of one species requires the death of individuals from other species. Although species-specific coevolution is easily identifiable (e.g., yucca plants and the so-called yucca moths cannot reproduce without the other) it is rare, contrary to the widespread diffuse coevolution. In diffuse coevolution, species are influenced by a wide variety of predators, parasites, preys, and mutualists.

Coevolution has served as inspiration to propose a family of evolutionary algorithms capable of surmounting some of the limitations encountered by evolutionary computation. These coevolutionary algorithms deal particularly well with increasing requirements of complexity and modularity while keeping computational cost bounded.

In this chapter I present Fuzzy CoCo, an original approach which applies cooperative coevolution to tackle the fuzzy-modeling problem. I begin by presenting some general notions of coevolutionary computation in the next section. Then, in Section 3.2, I discuss cooperative coevolution. In Section 3.3 I present in detail Fuzzy CoCo, my coevolutionary fuzzy modeling approach. I finally illustrate in Section 3.4 some of the capabilities of Fuzzy CoCo by applying it to a well-known classification problem.

3.1 Coevolutionary Computation

Inspired by natural coevolution, artificial coevolution refers to the simultaneous evolution of two or more species with coupled fitness (i.e., the fitness of one in-

C.A. Peña Reyes: Coevolutionary Fuzzy Modeling, LNCS 3204, pp. 51–69, 2004.
© Springer-Verlag Berlin Heidelberg 2004

dividual depends on the fitness of individuals of other species and/or on its interaction with them) [95]. Such coupled evolution provides some advantages over non-coevolutionary approaches that render coevolution an interesting alternative when confronting certain problems. Among these advantages, we can mention [44,72,85]:

– Coevolution favors the discovery of complex solutions whenever complex solutions are required.
– Coevolution helps preserve genetic diversity.
– Coevolution favors computationally efficient fitness functions.
– Coevolution is suitable for parallel implementation.

Another multiple-population evolutionary approach is the island model [19,67] in which isolated populations—the islands—evolve separately with occasional migration between them. Such migration implies genetic exchange among individuals from different populations, thus violating the interspecific genetic isolation required by strict coevolution. There exist, however, some island-model approaches in which individuals from different islands share their fitness, becoming fitness-dependent on one another as in the coevolutionary paradigm, leading to specialized subpopulations which are not genetically isolated. The fitness-sharing schema might be either explicit or implicit [13].

Simplistically speaking, one can say that coevolving species can either compete (e.g., to obtain exclusivity on a limited resource) or cooperate (e.g., to gain access to some hard-to-attain resource). Below I present the main concepts involved in competitive coevolution. Cooperative coevolution is presented in more detail in Section 3.2 as it is the approach on which I base my work.

In a competitive-coevolutionary algorithm, the fitness of an individual is based on direct competition with individuals of other species, which in turn evolve separately in their own populations. Increased fitness of one of the species implies a diminution in the fitness of the other species. This evolutionary pressure tends to produce new strategies in the populations involved so as to maintain their chances of survival. This "arms race" ideally increases the capabilities of each species until they reach an optimum.

One of the competitive relationships that have inspired artificial coevolution is parasitism. In this case, the term host refers to the individual whose fitness is under evaluation, and parasites refer to the individuals that are testing the host (trying to weaken it, not to kill it). This approach has been used to evolve sorting networks [31] and neural classifiers [72]. In other competitive approaches, two different species competing for the access to a limited resource (usually complementary fitness value) develop survival strategies in order to perform better than each other. This approach has been used to evolve artificial game players for Nim and three-dimensional tic-tac-toe [95], and to model predator-prey interaction in evolutionary robotics experiments [68].

3.2 Cooperative Coevolution

In nature, many species have developed cooperative interactions with other species to improve their survival. Such cooperative—also called mutualistic or symbiotic—coevolution can be found in organisms going from cells (e.g., eukaryotic organisms resulted probably from the mutualistic interaction between prokaryotes and some cells they infected) to superior animals (e.g., African tick birds obtain a steady food supply by cleaning parasites from the skin of giraffes, zebras, and other animals), including the common mutualism between plants and animals (e.g., pollination and seed dispersion in change of food) [90].

Cooperative coevolutionary algorithms involve a number of independently evolving species which together form complex structures, well-suited to solve a problem. The fitness of an individual depends on its ability to collaborate with individuals from other species. In this way, the evolutionary pressure stemming from the difficulty of the problem favors the development of cooperative strategies and individuals. As in nature the species are genetically isolated because they evolve in separate populations, because their genomes are genetically incompatible, or both.

3.2.1 Issues Addressed by Cooperative Coevolution

Single-population evolutionary algorithms often perform poorly—manifesting stagnation, convergence to local optima, and computational costliness—when confronted with problems presenting one or more of the following features:

1. The sought-after solution is *complex*.
2. The problem or its solution is *clearly decomposable*.
3. The genome encodes different *types of values*.
4. Strong *interdependencies* among the components of the solution.
5. *Components-ordering* drastically affects fitness.

Cooperative coevolution addresses effectively these issues, consequently widening the range of applications of evolutionary computation [85, 88]. Indeed, the coevolution of several species facilitates the existence of specialized individuals dealing with a subtask of a *complex* problem. The decomposition of the problem can be either user-designed in the case of *clearly decomposable* problems or emergent otherwise. As each species evolve separately, one can tailor the evolutionary algorithm controlling evolution to the specificities of the subtask, including a representation adapted to the *type of values* involved in the corresponding species. Finally, cooperative coevolution can be robust in face of the strong effects that *interdependencies* and *component-ordering* might have on fitness. In fact, as each individual has the possibility to cooperate several times, the chance that a good component disappears due to a destructive genetic operation on another component is lower than in single-population evolution.

3.2.2 Ancestral Work

To my knowledge, cooperative coevolution was applied for the first time by Husbands and Mill [38] to a highly generalized version of the manufacturing planning problem. This problem involves finding an optimal way to interleave a number of concurrent process plans which share resources. The optimization problem consists of simultaneously optimizing the individual process plans and the overall schedule. In their approach, Husbands and Mill evolve one species per process plan, together with an additional species of "Arbitrators" in charge of making decisions to deal with conflicts. The final fitness of each individual is calculated in two stages. The first stage involves local criteria and the second stage takes into account interactions between populations.

Potter and De Jong [85, 86, 88] developed a general model for cooperative coevolution in which a number of populations explore different decompositions of the problem. They explored their approach by applying it to different complex problems such as function optimization [86], neural network design [87], and the learning of sequential decision rules [89]. Section 3.2.3 detail this framework as it forms the basis of my own approach.

Paredis [72] applied cooperative coevolution to problems which involved finding simultaneously the values of a solution and their adequate order. In his approach, a population of solutions coevolves alongside a population of permutations performed on the genotypes of the solutions. Paredis used as test problem the solution of n random linear equations with different levels of coupling between the variables (i.e., with different difficulty levels).

Eriksson [17] applied cooperative coevolution to optimize the parameters controlling the inventory in a factory. This problem involves finding a set of parameters defining policies to control the stock of several items composing the inventory. Eriksson investigated two different ways to define the coevolving species. In the first representation, each individual encodes the values of one parameter for all the items, while in the second representation, each individual encodes all the parameters of a single inventory item. His results show that the latter representation exhibits some advantages over the former as it expresses better the interdependencies between the parameters.

Moriarty [63] used a cooperative coevolutionary approach to evolve neural networks. Each individual in one species corresponds to a single hidden neuron of a neural network and its connections with the input and output layers. This population coevolves alongside a second one whose individuals encode sets of hidden neurons (i.e., individuals from the first population) forming a neural network.

3.2.3 A General Model for Cooperative Coevolution

As mentioned before, Potter and De Jong [85, 88] developed a general model for cooperative coevolution. Their hypothesis was that explicit notions of modularity are necessary in order to evolve complex structures in the form of interacting coadapted subcomponents.

Their model has the following characteristics:

1. Each species represents a subcomponent of a potential solution.
2. Complete solutions are obtained by assembling *representative* members of each of the species (populations).
3. The fitness of each individual depends on the quality of the complete solutions it participated in, thus measuring how well it cooperates to solve the problem.
4. The evolution of each species is controlled by a separate, independent evolutionary algorithm.
5. Given an ensemble of conditions, the number of species should itself be adapted by a mechanism of birth and death of species.

Figure 3.1 shows the general architecture of Potter's cooperative coevolutionary framework, and the way each evolutionary algorithm computes the fitness of its individuals by combining them with selected representatives from the other species. The representatives can be selected via a greedy strategy as the fittest individuals from the last generation.

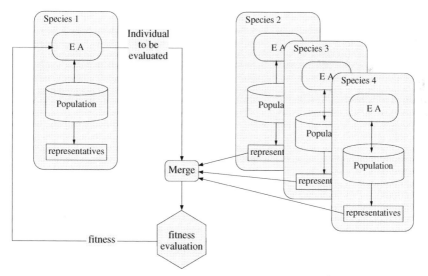

Fig. 3.1. Potter's cooperative coevolutionary system. The figure shows the evolutionary process from the perspective of Species 1. The individual being evaluated is combined with one or more *representatives* of the other species so as to construct several solutions which are tested on the problem. The individual's fitness depends on the quality of these solutions.

Results presented by Potter and De Jong [88] show that their approach addresses adequately issues like problem decomposition and interdependencies between subcomponents. The cooperative coevolutionary approach performs as good as, and sometimes better than, single-population evolutionary algorithms. Finally, cooperative coevolution usually requires less computation than single-population evolution as the populations involved are smaller, and convergence—in terms of number of generations—is faster.

3.3 Fuzzy CoCo

Fuzzy CoCo is a Cooperative Coevolutionary approach to fuzzy modeling wherein two coevolving species are defined: database (membership functions) and rule base. This approach is based primarily on the framework defined by Potter and De Jong [85, 88] (Section 3.2). Fuzzy CoCo is conceived to allow a high degree of freedom in the type of fuzzy systems it can design in order to allow the user to manage the trade-off between performance and interpretability.

A fuzzy modeling process needs usually deal with the simultaneous search for operational and connective parameters (Table 2.1). These parameters provide an almost complete definition of the linguistic knowledge describing the behavior of a fuzzy system, and of the values mapping this symbolic description into a real-valued world (a complete definition also requires structural parameters, such as relevant variables and number of rules). Thus, fuzzy modeling can be thought of as two separate but intertwined search processes: (1) the search for the membership functions (i.e., operational parameters) that define the fuzzy variables, and (2) the search for the rules (i.e., connective parameters) used to perform the inference.

Fuzzy modeling presents several features discussed in Section 3.2 which justify the application of cooperative coevolution: (1) The required solutions can be very complex, since fuzzy systems with a few dozen variables may call for hundreds of parameters to be defined. (2) The proposed solution—a fuzzy inference system—can be decomposed into two distinct components: rules and membership functions. (3) Membership functions are represented by continuous, real values, while rules are represented by discrete, symbolic values. (4) These two components are interdependent because the membership functions defined by the first group of values are indexed by the second group (rules).

Consequently, in Fuzzy CoCo, the fuzzy modeling problem is solved by two coevolving, cooperating species. Individuals of the first species encode values which define completely all the membership functions for all the variables of the system. For example, with respect to the variable *Triglycerides* shown in Figure 2.1, this problem is equivalent to finding the values of P_1, P_2, and P_3.

Individuals of the second species define a set of rules of the form:

if $(v_1$ **is** $A_1)$ **and ... and** $(v_n$ **is** $A_n)$ **then** $(output$ **is** $C)$,

where the term A_i indicates which one of the linguistic labels of fuzzy variable v is used by the rule. For example, a valid rule could contain the expression

if ... and $(Temperature$ **is** $Warm)$ **and ... then ...**

which includes the membership function $Warm$ whose defining parameters are contained in the first species.

3.3.1 The Algorithm

The two evolutionary algorithms used to control the evolution of the two populations are instances of a simple genetic algorithm [113]. Figure 3.2 presents the Fuzzy CoCo algorithm in pseudo-code format. The genetic algorithms apply fitness-proportionate selection to choose the mating pool (essentially, probabilistic selection according to fitness), and apply an elitist strategy with an elitism rate Er to allow some of the best individuals to survive into the next generation. The elitism strategy extracts E_S individuals—the so-called elite—to be reinserted into the population after evolutionary operators have been applied (i.e., selection, crossover, and mutation). Note that the elite is not removed from the population, participating thus in the reproduction process. Standard crossover and mutation operators are applied [60]: crossover between two genomes is performed with probability P_c by selecting at random (with uniform probability) a single crossover point and exchanging the subsequent parts to form two new offspring; if no crossover takes place (with probability $1 - P_c$) the two offspring are exact copies of their parents. Mutation involves flipping bits in the genome with probability P_m per bit. The condition under which the algorithm terminates is usually satisfied either when a given threshold fitness is attained, or when the maximum number of generations, G_{max}, is reached.

```
begin Fuzzy CoCo
    g:=0
    for each species S
        Initialize populations P_S(0)
        Evaluate population P_S(0)
    end for
    while not done do
        for each species S
            g:=g+1
            E_S(g) = Elite-select[P_S(g − 1)]
            P'_S(g) = Select[P_S(g − 1)]
            P''_S(g) = Crossover[P'_S(g)]
            P'''_S(g) = Mutate[P''_S(g)]
            P_S(g) = P'''_S(g) + E_S(g)
            Evaluate population P_S(g)
        end for
    end while
end Fuzzy CoCo
```

Fig. 3.2. Pseudo-code of Fuzzy CoCo. Two species coevolve in Fuzzy CoCo: membership functions and rules. The elitism strategy extracts E_S individuals to be reinserted into the population after evolutionary operators have been applied (i.e., selection, crossover, and mutation). Selection results in a reduced population $P'_S(g)$ (usually, the size of $P'_S(g)$ is $\|P'_S\| = \|P_S\| - \|E_S\|$). The line "Evaluate population $P_S(g)$" is elaborated in Figure 3.3.

3.3.2 Elitism

I introduced elitism to avoid the divergent behavior of Fuzzy CoCo, observed in preliminary trial runs. Contrary to Juillé's statement about premature convergence of cooperative coevolution [44]—due in his case to the fact that he was searching for solution-test pairs, two inherently competitive species—non-elitist versions of Fuzzy CoCo often tend to lose the genetic information of good individuals found during evolution, consequently producing populations with mediocre individuals scattered throughout the search space. This is probably due to the relatively small size of the populations which renders difficult the preservation (exploitation) of good solutions while exploring the search space.

The introduction of simple elitism produces an undesirable effect on Fuzzy CoCo's performance: populations converge prematurely even with reduced values of the elitism rate E_r. To offset this effect without losing the advantages of elitism, it is necessary to increase the mutation probability P_m by an order of magnitude so as to improve the exploration capabilities of the algorithm. As the dispersion effect is less important when Fuzzy CoCo is allowed to manage relatively large populations, the values of both E_r and P_m should be reduced in such case.

3.3.3 Fitness Evaluation

A more detailed view of the fitness evaluation process is depicted in Figure 3.3. An individual undergoing fitness evaluation establishes cooperations with one or more representatives of the other species, i.e., it is combined with individuals from the other species to construct fuzzy systems. The fitness value assigned to the individual depends on the performance of the fuzzy systems it participated in (specifically, either the average or the maximal value).

Representatives, or *cooperators*, are selected both fitness-proportionally and randomly from the last generation in which they were already assigned a fitness value (see Figure 3.2). In Fuzzy CoCo, N_{cf} cooperators are selected probabilistically according to their fitness, favoring the fittest individuals, thus boosting the exploitation of known good solutions. The other N_{cr} cooperators are selected randomly from the population to represent the diversity of the species, maintaining in this way exploration of the search space.

3.3.4 Interpretability Considerations

As mentioned before, Fuzzy CoCo allows a high degree of freedom in the type of fuzzy systems it can design, letting the user determine the accuracy-interpretability trade-off. When the interest is to preserve as much as possible the interpretability of the evolved systems, the fuzzy model should satisfy the semantic and syntactic criteria presented in Section 2.3. The mentioned strategies—label sharing, orthogonal membership functions, don't-care conditions, and default rule—must guide both the design of the fuzzy inference system and the definition of both species' genomes.

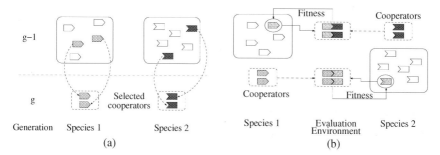

Fig. 3.3. Fitness evaluation in Fuzzy CoCo. (a) Several individuals from generation $g - 1$ of each species are selected both randomly and according to their fitness to be the representatives of their species during generation g; these representatives are called "cooperators." (b) During the evaluation stage of generation g (after selection, crossover, and mutation—see Figure 3.2), individuals are combined with the selected cooperators of the other species to construct fuzzy systems. These systems are then evaluated on the problem domain and serve as a basis for assigning the final fitness to the individual being evaluated.

Note that the existence of one separated species representing membership functions in Fuzzy CoCo, already implements the label-sharing strategy.

Besides, one or more of the linguistic criteria may participate in the fitness function as a way to reinforce the selection pressure towards interpretable systems. The example presented in the next section illustrates both the application of Fuzzy CoCo and the way interpretability criteria are introduced in it.

3.3.5 Other Cooperative Coevolutionary Approaches to Fuzzy Modeling

Apart from Fuzzy CoCo, the use of cooperative coevolution to develop fuzzy models is scarce and the few existing works limit themselves to a brief description and do not develop a structured approach nor study the characteristics of the proposed algorithms. Because of that, I can can cautiously claim that Fuzzy CoCo is the first consistent work in cooperative coevolutionary fuzzy modeling.

The earliest work reporting on coevolution for building fuzzy systems does not fit strictly the conditions to be considered as coevolutionary. Indeed, in their approach, Włoszek and Domański [117, 118], describe an island-based evolutionary system implementing in each island a Michigan-type modeling process (Section 2.2.2). After each evolutionary step, they allow the populations to exchange rules using an aggressive migration policy—up to 25% of the rule base.

In 1997, Hopf [36] applied Potter's coevolutionary model [85, 86] to build the rule base of a fuzzy system. In his approach, Hopf implements a species for each rule composing the rule base. A candidate rule base is thus formed by an individual of each species. The pre-defined membership functions are distributed regularly over each variable's universe of discourse. This behavior-learning approach (Section 2.2.1) is applied to approximate an abstract function obtaining results that compare favorably with those of a simple genetic algorithm.

Jun, Joung, and Sim [45] applied a method, similar to Fuzzy CoCo in that it implements two species encoding, respectively, rules and membership functions. They applied different evolutionary algorithms to control each species evolution: (1) a discrete alphabet representation with $(\mu + \lambda)$ selection and no crossover operator for the rule species, and (2) a simple genetic algorithm with binary representation for the membership-function species. They applied their approach to design a fuzzy controller for the navigation of two simulated mobile robots which "find their goal positions in relatively short time and avoid obstacles successfully". The main difference between their approach and Fuzzy CoCo is the fitness evaluation stage and the associated computational cost. While the evaluation of each individual in Fuzzy CoCo is based on a reduced number of cooperating relations (i.e., $N_{cf} + N_{cr}$); each individual in their approach must cooperate with every individual in the other population to obtain its fitness. The cost of this meticulous exploration is a huge computational load.

Two more recent works have applied cooperative coevolution to design fuzzy controllers. Both Jeong and Oh [41] and Juang, Lin, and Lin [43] implement a species-per-rule strategy in which each individual represents a single rule defined by its own input and output membership functions. As usual in fuzzy-control applications, where the number of involved variables is low, these two works neglect interpretability in favor of precision. Note that Juang, Lin, and Lin select only random cooperators (i.e., $N_{cf} = 0$), while Jeong and Oh select only the fittest individual as cooperators (i.e., $N_{cf} = 1$ and $N_{cr} = 0$).

3.4 Application Example: The Iris Problem

Applying Fuzzy CoCo requires the definition of parameters of its two main components: (1) the fuzzy system and (2) the cooperative coevolutionary algorithm (Section 5.1 discusses in more detail the application of Fuzzy CoCo). Some of the fuzzy-system parameters must be pre-defined according to the available a-priori knowledge, and the remaining parameters are considered targets for the evolutionary algorithm. As for the cooperative-coevolution parameters, the designer needs to define the maximum number of generations, the population size, the number of cooperators, and the crossover, mutation, and elitism rates. In the fuzzy systems evolved in the present chapter, I applied Fuzzy CoCo with the same evolutionary parameters for both species. To illustrate the application of Fuzzy CoCo, I present in the following subsections the evolution of two different fuzzy systems to solve a hard classification problem.

3.4.1 Fisher's Iris Data

Fisher's Iris data is a well-known classification problem consisting of feature measurements for the speciation of iris flowers [5, 20]. There are three classes corresponding to three species of iris: *setosa*, *versicolor*, and *virginica*, where each flower can be identified according to four continuous attributes measured in centimeters: (1) sepal length (SL); (2) sepal width (SW), (3) petal length (PL), and (4) petal width (PW). The 150 database entries include 50 sample cases for each of the three species. The goal is to classify irises into one of the three classes in accordance with the four inputs. To illustrate the distribution of the iris data, Figure 3.4 depicts all the 150 entries in the bidimensional subspace defined by variables PL and PW.

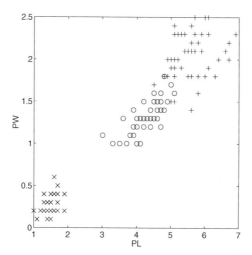

Fig. 3.4. Iris data distribution in the PL–PW subspace. The three classes: *setosa*, *versicolor*, and *virginica* correspond to marks **x**, **o**, and **+**, respectively. The fact that almost all the *versicolor* cases are in between *setosa* and *virginica* cases can be exploited for the design of classification systems.

Fisher's iris data has been widely used to test classification and modeling algorithms, recently including fuzzy models [35, 37, 96, 105, 119]. I propose herein two types of fuzzy logic-based systems to solve the iris data classification problem: (1) fuzzy controller-type (as used by Shi *et al.* [105] and Russo [96]), and (2) fuzzy classifier-type (as used by Hong and Chen [35], Hung and Lin [37], and Wu and Chen [119]). Both types consist of a fuzzy inference system and a selection unit.

In the fuzzy controller (see Figure 3.5) the fuzzy subsystem computes a single continuous value estimating the class to which the input vector belongs. Note that each class is assigned a numeric value; based on the iris data distribution, I assigned values 1, 2, and 3 to the classes *setosa*, *versicolor*, and *virginica*, respectively (such an assignment makes sense only under the assumption that *versicolor* is an intermediate species in between *setosa* and *virginica*, see Figure 3.4). The selection unit approximates this value to the nearest class value using a stair function.

In the fuzzy classifier (see Figure 3.6) the fuzzy inference subsystem computes a continuous membership value for each class. The selection unit chooses the most active class, provided that its membership value exceeds a given threshold (which I set to 0.5).

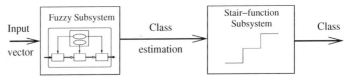

Fig. 3.5. Fuzzy controller used to solve Fisher's iris data problem. The fuzzy subsystem is used to compute a continuous value that describes the class to which a given input vector belongs (the three classes: *setosa*, *versicolor*, and *virginica* correspond to values 1, 2, and 3, respectively). The stair-function approximates the computed value to the nearest class value.

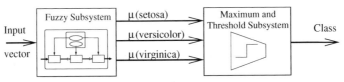

Fig. 3.6. Fuzzy classifier used to solve Fisher's iris data problem. The fuzzy subsystem is used to compute the membership value of a given input vector for each of the three classes: *setosa*, *versicolor*, and *virginica*. The maximum-and-threshold subsystem chooses the class with the maximum membership value, provided this value exceeds a given threshold.

The two fuzzy subsystems thus differ in the number of output variables: a single output (with values $\{1,2,3\}$) for the controller-type and three outputs (with values $\{0,1\}$) for the classifier-type. In general, controller-type systems take advantage of data distribution while classifier-type systems offer higher interpretability because the output classes are independent; these latter systems are harder to design.

3.4.2 Application of Fuzzy CoCo to the Iris Problem

I used prior knowledge about the iris data problem and about some of the fuzzy systems proposed in the literature for its solution to guide my choice of fuzzy parameters. In addition, I took into account the interpretability criteria presented in Section 2.3 to define constraints on the fuzzy parameters. Referring to Table 2.1, I delineate below the fuzzy system's set-up:

- *Logical parameters:* singleton-type fuzzy systems; min-max fuzzy operators; orthogonal, trapezoidal-triangular input membership functions (see Figure 3.7); weighted-average defuzzification.
- *Structural parameters:* three input membership functions (*Low*, *Medium*, and *High*); three output singletons for the controller-type system and two output singletons for the classifier-type system; a user-configurable number of rules. The relevant variables are one of Fuzzy CoCo's evolutionary objectives.
- *Connective parameters:* the antecedents and the consequent of the rules are searched by Fuzzy CoCo. The algorithm also searches for the consequent of the default rule. All rules have unitary weight.

– *Operational parameters:* the input membership function values are to be found by Fuzzy CoCo. For the output singletons I used the values 1, 2, and 3 for the controller-type system, and the values 0 and 1 for the classifier-type system.

Fuzzy CoCo thus searches for four parameters: input membership-function values, relevant input variables, and antecedents and consequents of rules. The genomes of the two species are constructed as follows:

– Species 1: Membership functions. There are four variables (SL, SW, PL, and PW), each with three parameters P_1, P_2, and P_3, defining the membership-function edges (Figure 3.7).

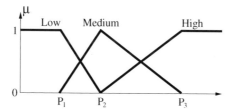

Fig. 3.7. Input fuzzy variables for the iris problem. Each fuzzy variable has three possible fuzzy values labeled **Low**, **Medium**, and **High**, and orthogonal membership functions, plotted above as degree of membership versus input value. Parameters P_1, P_2, and P_3 define the membership-function edges.

– Species 2: Rules (Controller-type systems). The i-th rule has the form:
    if (SL **is** A^i_{SL}) **and ... and** (PW **is** A^i_{PW}) **then** (*output* **is** C^i),
A^i_j can take on the values: 1 (*Low*), 2 (*Medium*), 3 (*High*), or 0 (*Don't Care*). C^i can take on the values: 1 (*setosa*), 2 (*versicolor*), or 3 (*virginica*). Relevant variables are searched for implicitly by allowing the algorithm to choose the *Don't Care* label (i.e., $A^i_j = 0$) as valid antecedents; in such case the respective variable is considered irrelevant, and is removed from the rule. The default rule is defined by its consequent parameter C^0.
– Species 2: Rules (Classifier-type systems). The i-th rule has the form:
    if (SL **is** A^i_{SL}) **and ... and** (PW **is** A^i_{PW})
    then {(*setosa* **is** C^i_{set}), (*versicolor* **is** C^i_{ver}), (*virginica* **is** C^i_{vir})},
A^i_j can take on the values: 1 (*Low*), 2 (*Medium*), 3 (*High*), or 0 (*Other*). C^i_j can take on the values: 0 (*No*), or 1 (*Yes*). Relevant variables are searched for implicitly by allowing the algorithm to choose non-existent membership functions (i.e., $A^i_j = 0$) as valid antecedents; in such case the respective variable is considered irrelevant, and is removed from the rule. The default rule is defined by its consequent parameters C^0_{set}, C^0_{ver}, and C^0_{vir}.

Table 3.1 delineates the parameters encoding both species' genomes, which together describe an entire fuzzy system.

Table 3.2 delineates values and ranges of values of the evolutionary parameters. The algorithm terminates when the maximum number of generations, G_{max},

Table 3.1. Genome encoding of parameters for both species. Genome length for Species 1 (membership functions) is 60 bits. Genome length for Species 2 (rules) is $10 \times N_r + 2$ for the controller-type system and $11 \times N_r + 3$ for the classifier-type system, where N_r denotes the number of rules. Values V_{min} and V_{max} for parameters P_i are defined according to the ranges of the four variables SL, SW, PL, and PW.

Species 1: Membership functions

Parameter	Values	Bits	Qty	Total bits
P_i	$[V_{min} - V_{max}]$	5	3×4	60

Species 2: Rules (Controller-type)

Parameter	Values	Bits	Qty	Total bits
A^i_j	$\{0,1,2,3\}$	2	$4 \times N_r$	$8 \times N_r$
C^i	$\{1,2,3\}$	2	$N_r + 1$	$2 \times (N_r + 1)$
		Total Genome Length		$10 \times N_r + 2$

Species 2: Rules (Classifier-type)

Parameter	Values	Bits	Qty	Total bits
A^i_j	$\{0,1,2,3\}$	2	$4 \times N_r$	$8 \times N_r$
C^i_j	$\{0,1\}$	1	$3 \times (N_r + 1)$	$3 \times (N_r + 1)$
		Total Genome Length		$11 \times N_r + 3$

is reached (I set $G_{max} = 500 + 100 \times N_r$, i.e., dependent on the number of rules used in the run), or when the increase in fitness of the best individual over five successive generations falls below a certain threshold (10^{-4} in my experiments). Note that mutation rates are relatively higher than with a simple genetic algorithm, which is typical of coevolutionary algorithms [85, 88]. This is due in part to the small population sizes and to elitism.

Table 3.2. Fuzzy CoCo set-up. Population size was fixed to 60 for controller-type systems and to 70 for classifier-type systems.

Parameter	Values
Population size $\|P_S\|$	$\{60,70\}$
Maximum generations G_{max}	$500 + 100 \times N_r$
Crossover probability P_c	1
Mutation probability P_m	$\{0.02,0.05,0.1\}$
Elitism rate E_r	$\{0.1,0.2\}$
"Fit" cooperators N_{cf}	1
Random cooperators N_{cr}	$\{1,2\}$

My fitness function combines three criteria: (1) F_c: classification performance, computed as the percentage of cases correctly classified; (2) F_{mse}: a value dependent on the mean square error (mse), measured between the continuous values of the outputs and the correct classification given by the iris data set ($F_{mse} = 1 - mse$); and (3) F_v: a rule-length dependent fitness equal 0 when the average number of variables per active rule is maximal and equal 1 in the hypothetical case of zero-length rules. The fitness function, defined as follows, combines these three measures:

$$F = \begin{cases} F_c \times F_{mse}^{\beta} & \text{if } F_c < 1 \\ (F_c - \alpha F_v) \times F_v^{\beta} & \text{if } F_c = 1, \end{cases}$$

where $\alpha = 1/150$ and $\beta = 0.3$. F_c, the ratio of correctly classified samples, is the most important measure of performance. F_{mse} adds selection pressure towards systems with low quadratic error, in which misclassifications are closer to "crossing the line" and becoming correct classifications. F_v measures the interpretability, penalizing systems with a large number of variables per rule (on average). F_v penalization is only applied to perfect classifiers as the number of variables in the iris data problem is low and 100% classification rate can be attained. The value β was set small enough to penalize systems exhibiting a large quadratic error. The value α was calculated to allow F_v to penalize rule multiplicity, but without decreasing fitness to a value below lower-performance systems.

3.4.3 Results

In this section I present the fuzzy systems evolved using Fuzzy CoCo for the two setups described above. I compare my systems with those presented in recently published articles, which thus represent the state-of-the-art. I detail some high-performance systems obtained for each problem in order to illustrate the type of systems found by Fuzzy CoCo.

3.4.3.1 Controller-Type Systems. I performed a total of 145 evolutionary runs, searching for controller-type systems with 2, 3, and 4 rules, all of which found systems whose classification performance exceeds 97.33% (i.e., the worst system misclassifies only 4 cases). The average classification performance of these runs was 98.98%, corresponding to 1.5 misclassifications. 121 runs led to a fuzzy system misclassifying 2 or less cases, and of these, 4 runs found perfect classifiers. Figure 3.8 summarizes my results.

Table 3.3 compares my best controller-type systems with the top systems obtained by two other evolutionary fuzzy modeling approaches. Shi *et al.* [105] used a simple genetic algorithm with adaptive crossover and adaptive mutation operators. Russo's FuGeNeSys method [96] combines evolutionary algorithms and neural networks to produce fuzzy systems. The search power of this latter method lies mainly in artificial evolution, while neural-based learning techniques are applied only to improve the performance of promising (high-performance) systems. The main drawback of these two methods is the low interpretability of the generated systems. As they do not define constraints on the input membership-function shapes, almost none of the semantic criteria presented in Section 2.3 are respected.

As evident in Table 3.3, the evolved fuzzy systems described in this section surpass or equal those obtained by the two other approaches in terms of performance, while maintaining high interpretability. Thus, my approach not only produces systems exhibiting high performance, but also ones with less rules and less antecedents per rule (which systems are thus more interpretable).

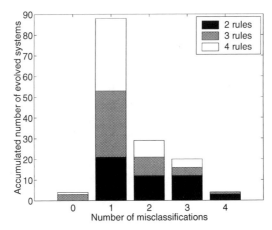

Fig. 3.8. Summary of results of 145 Fuzzy CoCo runs searching for controller-type systems. The histogram depicts the total number of systems for a given number of misclassifications, at the end of the Fuzzy CoCo run.

Table 3.3. Comparison of the best controller-type systems evolved by Fuzzy CoCo with the top fuzzy systems obtained by Russo's FuGeNeSys method [96] and with those obtained using a single-population evolutionary approach by Shi et al. [105]. Shown below are the classification rates of the top systems obtained by these approaches, along with the average number of variables per rule in parentheses. Results are divided into four classes, in accordance with the number of rules per system, going from two-rule systems to five-rule ones. The highlighted system is the top-performance one, detailed in Figure 3.9. A dash implies that the relevant system was not designed.

Rules per system	Shi et al. [105] best	FuGeNeSys [96] best	Fuzzy CoCo average	best
2	–	–	98.71% (1.9)	99.33% (2)
3	–	–	99.10% (1.3)	**100% (1.7)**
4	98.00% (2.6)	–	99.12% (1.3)	100% (2.5)
5	–	100% (3.3)	–	–

Fuzzy CoCo found controller-type systems with 3 and 4 rules exhibiting perfect performance (no misclassifications). Among these, I consider as best the system with fewest rules and variables. Figure 3.9 presents one such three-rule system, with an average of 1.7 variables per rule.

3.4.3.2 Classifier-Type Systems. I performed a total of 144 evolutionary runs, searching for controller-type systems with 2, 3, and 4 rules, all of which found systems whose classification performance exceeds 95.33% (i.e., the worst system misclassifies 7 cases). The average classification performance of these runs was 97.40%, corresponding to 3.9 misclassifications. 104 runs led to a fuzzy system misclassifying 5 or less cases, and of these, 13 runs found systems with a single misclassification. Figure 3.10 summarizes these results.

Table 3.4 compares my best classifier-type systems [76] with the top systems obtained by three other fuzzy modeling approaches. Hong and Chen [35] and Wu and

Database				
	SL	*SW*	*PL*	*PW*
P_1	5.68	3.16	1.19	1.55
P_2	6.45	3.16	1.77	1.65
P_3	7.10	3.45	6.03	1.74

Rule base

Rule 1	**if** (*PL* **is** *High*) **then** (*output* **is** *virginica*)
Rule 2	**if** (*SW* **is** *Low*) **and** (*PW* **is** *High*) **then** (*output* **is** *virginica*)
Rule 3	**if** (*SL* **is** *Medium*) **and** (*PW* **is** *Medium*) **then** (*output* **is** *setosa*)
Default	**else** (*output* **is** *setosa*)

Fig. 3.9. The best evolved, controller-type system with three rules. It exhibits a classification rate of 100%, and an average of 1.7 variables per rule. Note that there is no rule classifying explicitly for *versicolor* class. The system interprets as *versicolor* cases where rules classifying both *setosa* and *virginica* classes have similar activation levels. For example, if the activation level is 0.5 for both classes 1 (*setosa*) and 3 (*virginica*), then the defuzzifier will output 2 (*versicolor*).

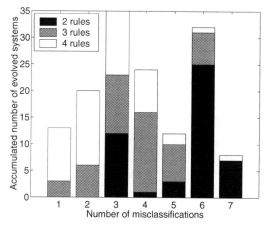

Fig. 3.10. Summary of results of 144 Fuzzy CoCo runs searching for classifier-type systems. The histogram depicts the total number of systems for a given number of misclassifications, at the end of the Fuzzy CoCo run.

Chen [119] proposed constructive learning methods (Section 2.1.2.3) to progressively construct their fuzzy systems. The stages of their methods are very similar: find relevant attributes, build initial membership functions, simplify the attributes and the membership functions, and derive decision rules; the two works differ in the strategies implemented to perform each stage. Thanks to attribute-selection and simplification stages, these two approaches are able to find systems with either a few [119] or simple rules [35]. They do not, however, constrain the input membership functions, thus rendering the obtained systems less interpretable. Hung and Lin [37] proposed a neuro-fuzzy hybrid approach to learn classifier-type systems. As their learning strategy hinges mainly on the adaptation of the connection weights, their systems exhibit low interpretability.

The evolved fuzzy systems described herein surpass or equal those obtained by these three approaches in terms of both performance and interpretability. As evident in Table 3.4, my approach not only produces systems exhibiting higher performance, but also ones with less rules and less antecedents per rule (which are thus more interpretable).

Table 3.4. Comparison of the best classifier-type systems evolved by Fuzzy CoCo with systems obtained applying constructive learning methods proposed by Hong and Chen [35] and by Wu and Chen [119], and with those obtained by Hung and Lin's neuro-fuzzy approach [37]. Shown below are the classification rates of the top systems obtained by these approaches, along with the average number of variables per rule in parentheses. Results are divided into four classes, in accordance with the number of rules per system, going from two-rule systems to eight-rule ones. The highlighted system is the top-performance one, detailed in Figure 3.11. A dash implies that the relevant system was not designed.

Rules per system	Hong and Chen [35]	Wu and Chen [119]	Hung and Lin [37]	Fuzzy CoCo	
	best	average	average	average	best
2	–	–	–	96.47% (2.1)	98.00% (1.5)
3	–	96.21% (4)	–	97.51% (2.4)	**99.33% (2.3)**
4	–	–	97.40% (4)	98.21% (2.3)	99.33% (2)
8	97.33% (2)	–	–	–	–

Fuzzy CoCo found classifier-type systems with 3 and 4 rules exhibiting the highest classification performance to date (i.e., 99.33%, corresponding to 1 misclassification). I consider as most interesting the system with the smallest number of conditions (i.e., the total number of variables in the rules). Figure 3.11 presents one such system. This three-rule system presents an average of 2.3 variables per rule, corresponding to a total of 7 conditions.

Database				
	SL	SW	PL	PW
P_1	4.65	2.68	4.68	0.39
P_2	4.65	3.74	5.26	1.16
P_3	5.81	4.61	6.03	2.03

Rule base

Rule 1   **if** (PW **is** *Low*)
          then {(*setosa* **is** *Yes*), (*versicolor* **is** *No*), (*virginica* **is** *No*) }
Rule 2   **if** (PL **is** *Low*) **and** (PW **is** *Medium*)
          then{(*setosa* **is** *No*), (*versicolor* **is** *Yes*), (*virginica* **is** *No*)}
Rule 3   **if** (SL **is** *High*) **and** (SW **is** *Medium*) **and** (PL **is** *Low*) **and** (PW **is** *High*)
          then{(*setosa* **is** *No*), (*versicolor* **is** *Yes*), (*virginica* **is** *No*)}
Default   **else**{(*setosa* **is** *No*), (*versicolor* **is** *No*), (*virginica* **is** *Yes*)}

Fig. 3.11. The best evolved, classifier-type system with three rules. It exhibits a classification rate of 99.33%, and an average of 2.3 variables per rule.

The high performance exhibited by these systems should suggest the presence of overfitting (i.e, the system adapts so well to the training set that it incorporates data disturbances in the model). However, a thorough generality analysis, presented in Section 5.4, shows that the best systems found do not have very-specific rules (i.e., rules that have learnt exceptions instead of patterns).

3.5 Summary

In this chapter I presented a novel approach to fuzzy modeling based on cooperative coevolution. The method, called Fuzzy CoCo, involves the existence of two separated coevolving species: rules and membership functions. A greedy fitness evaluation strategy, based on the use of selected cooperators from each species, allows the method to balance adequately the exploration and the exploitation of the search while keeping bounded the computational cost.

I propose Fuzzy CoCo as a methodology for modeling fuzzy systems and have conceived it to allow a high degree of freedom in the type of fuzzy systems it can design. Fuzzy CoCo can be used to model Mamdani-type, TSK-type, and singleton-type fuzzy models2.1. The rules can contain an arbitrary number of antecedents (i.e., zero, one, or many) for the same variable. The designer is free to choose the type of membership functions used for each variable and the way they are parameterized. The membership functions can be defined either as shared by all fuzzy rules, or per-rule. Fuzzy CoCo is thus highly general and generic.

The configurability of Fuzzy CoCo facilitates the management of the interpretability-accuracy trade-off. To satisfy interpretability criteria, the user must impose conditions on the input and output membership functions as well as on the rule definition. In Fuzzy CoCo these conditions are translated both into restrictions on the choice of fuzzy parameters and into criteria included in the fitness function.

I also illustrated the use of Fuzzy CoCo by applying it to a well-known classification problem: the Iris problem. Two types of fuzzy systems—controller-type and classifier-type—were successfully modelled to solve the problem. Further applications of Fuzzy CoCo to hard medical diagnosis problems are presented in the next chapter.

4 Breast Cancer Diagnosis by Fuzzy CoCo

Although computerized tools for medical diagnosis have been developed since the early 60s, their number and capabilities have grown impressively in the last years due, mainly, to the availability of medical data and increased computing power. Most of these systems are conceived to provide high diagnostic performance. However, interest has recently shifted to systems capable of providing, besides a correct diagnosis, insight on how the answer was obtained. Thanks to their linguistic representation and their numeric behavior, fuzzy systems can provide both performance and explanation.

In this chapter, I apply Fuzzy CoCo to model the decision processes involved in two breast-cancer diagnostic problems. First, I describe in Section 4.1, the application of Fuzzy CoCo to the Wisconsin Breast Cancer Diagnostic problem (already presented in Section 2.4). Then, in Section 4.2, I present the application of Fuzzy CoCo to the design of COBRA, a fuzzy-based tool to assess mammography interpretation.

4.1 Breast-Biopsy Analysis: The WBCD Problem

The Wisconsin Breast Cancer Diagnosis (WBCD) problem, already introduced in Section 2.4, involves classifying a presented case of putative cancer as to whether it is benign or malignant. It admits a relatively high number of variables and consequently a large search space. Recall that the WBCD database consists of 683 cases of breast biopsy evaluations. Each case has nine input attributes and a binary diagnostic output. The solution I propose for this problem consists of a fuzzy appraisal system and a threshold unit (see Figure 2.5). The goal is to evolve a fuzzy model that describes the diagnostic decision, while exhibiting both good classification performance and high interpretability. A detailed description of the WBCD problem is presented in Section 2.4.1.

4.1.1 The Evolutionary Setup

The system proposed to solve the WBCD problem, consisting of a fuzzy system and a threshold unit, is presented in Section 2.4.2. While Fuzzy CoCo might use the same fuzzy-system parameters defined for the fuzzy-genetic approach, the evolutionary setup must be redefined within the Fuzzy CoCo framework.

C.A. Peña Reyes: Coevolutionary Fuzzy Modeling, LNCS 3204, pp. 71-87, 2004.
© Springer-Verlag Berlin Heidelberg 2004

Fuzzy CoCo is used to search for four parameters: input membership-function values, relevant input variables, and antecedents and consequents of rules. These search goals are more ambitious than those defined for the fuzzy-genetic approach (Section 2.4.2) as the consequents of rules are added to the search space. The genomes of the two species are constructed as follows:

- Species 1: Membership functions. There are nine variables (v_1 – v_9), each with two parameters, P and d, defining the start point and the length of the membership-function edges, respectively (Figure 2.6).
- Species 2: Rules. The i-th rule has the form:
  if (v_1 **is** A_1^i) **and** ... **and** (v_9 **is** A_9^i) **then** (*output is* C^i),
  A_j^i can take on the values: 1 (*Low*), 2 (*High*), or 0 or 3 (*Don't Care*). C^i bit can take on the values: 0 (*Benign*) or 1 (*Malignant*). Relevant variables are searched for implicitly by letting the algorithm choose *Don't care* labels as valid antecedents; in such a case the respective variable is considered irrelevant.

Table 4.1 delineates the parameter encoding for both species' genomes, which together describe an entire fuzzy system. Note that in the fuzzy-genetic approach (Section 2.4.2) both membership functions and rules were encoded in the same genome, i.e., there was only one species.

Table 4.1. Genome encoding of parameters for both species. Genome length for membership functions is 54 bits. Genome length for rules is $19 \times N_r + 1$, where N_r denotes the number of rules.

Species 1: Membership functions

Parameter	Values	Bits	Qty	Total bits
P	$\{1,2,...,8\}$	3	9	27
d	$\{1,2,...,8\}$	3	9	27
	Total Genome Length			54

Species 2: Rules

Parameter	Values	Bits	Qty	Total bits
A	$\{0,1,2,3\}$	2	$9 \times N_r$	$18 \times N_r$
C	$\{1,2\}$	1	$N_r + 1$	$N_r + 1$
	Total Genome Length			$19 \times N_r + 1$

To evolve the fuzzy inference system, I applied Fuzzy CoCo with the same evolutionary parameters for both species. Table 4.2 delineates the values and ranges of values used for these parameters. The algorithm terminates when the maximum number of generations, G_{max}, is reached (I set $G_{max} = 1000 + 100 \times N_r$, i.e., dependent on the number of rules used in the run), or when the increase in fitness of the best individual over five successive generations falls below a certain threshold (10^{-4} in my experiments).

The fitness function combines two criteria: 1) F_c—classification performance, computed as the percentage of cases correctly classified, and 2) F_v—the maximum number of variables in the longest rule. The fitness function is given by

Table 4.2. Fuzzy CoCo set-up for the WBCD problem.

Parameter	Values
Population size $\|Ps\|$	[30-90]
Maximum generations G_{max}	$1000 + 100 N_r$
Crossover probability P_c	1
Mutation probability P_m	[0.02-0.3]
Elitism rate E_r	[0.1-0.6]
"Fit" co-operators N_{cf}	1
Random co-operators N_{cr}	{1,2,3,4}

$F = F_c - \alpha F_v$, where $\alpha = 0.0015$. F_c, the percentage of correctly diagnosed cases, is the most important measure of performance. F_v measures the interpretability, penalizing systems with a large number of variables in their rules. The value α was calculated to allow F_v to occasion a fitness difference only among systems exhibiting similar classification performance. The fitness value assigned to an individual is the maximum of the fitness values obtained by the N_c fuzzy systems it participated in (where $N_c = N_{cf} + N_{cr}$).

I stated earlier that cooperative coevolution reduces the computational cost of the search process. In order to measure this cost I calculated the maximum number of fuzzy-system evaluations performed by a single run of Fuzzy CoCo. Each generation, the $\|Ps\|$ individuals of each population are evaluated N_c times (where $N_c = N_{cf} + N_{cr}$). The total number of fuzzy-system evaluations per run is thus $2 \times G_{max} \times \|Ps\| \times N_c$. This value ranged from 5.28×10^5 evaluations for a one-rule system search, up to 8.16×10^5 evaluations for a seven-rule system (using typical parameter values: $\|Ps\| = 80$, $N_{cf} = 1$, and $N_{cr} = 2$). The number of fuzzy-system evaluations required by the single-population approach was, on the average, 5×10^5 for a one-rule system and 11×10^5 for a seven-rule system 2.4. This shows that Fuzzy CoCo produces markedly better results using similar computational resources.

4.1.2 Results

A total of 495 evolutionary runs were performed, all of which found systems whose classification performance exceeds 96.7%. In particular, considering the best individual per run (i.e., the evolved system with the highest classification success rate), 241 runs led to a fuzzy system whose performance exceeds 98.0%, and of these, 81 runs found systems whose performance exceeds 98.5%.; these results are summarized in Figure 4.1.

Table 4.3 compares the best systems found by Fuzzy CoCo with the top systems obtained by the fuzzy-genetic approach (Section 2.4) [75, 78] and with the systems obtained by Setiono's NeuroRule approach [102] (note that the results presented by these two works were the best reported to date for genetic-fuzzy and neuro-Boolean rule systems, respectively, and that they were compared with other previous approaches such as [101, 103, 107]). The evolved fuzzy systems described herein can

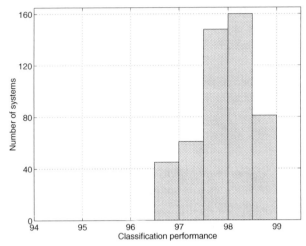

Fig. 4.1. Summary of results of 495 evolutionary runs. The histogram depicts the number of systems exhibiting a given performance level at the end of the evolutionary run. The performance considered is that of the best individual of the run, measured as the overall percentage of correctly classified cases over the entire database.

be seen to surpass those obtained by other approaches in terms of performance, while still containing simple, interpretable rules. As shown in Table 4.3, I obtained higher-performance systems for all rule-base sizes but one, i.e., from two-rule systems to seven-rule ones, while all my one-rule systems perform as well as the best system reported by Setiono.

Table 4.3. Comparison of the best systems evolved by Fuzzy CoCo with the top systems obtained using single-population evolution [75] and with those obtained by Setiono's NeuroRule approach [102]. Shown below are the classification performance values of the top systems obtained by these approaches, along with the number of variables of the longest rule in parentheses. Results are divided into seven classes, in accordance with the number of rules per system, going from one-rule systems to seven-rule ones.

Rules per system	Neuro-Rule [102]	Single population GA [75][a]	Fuzzy CoCo	
	best	best	average	best
1	97.36% (4)	97.07% (4)	97.36% (4)	97.36% (4)
2	–	97.36% (4)	97.73% (3.9)	98.54% (5)
3	98.10% (4)	97.80% (6)	97.91% (4.4)	98.54% (4)
4	–	97.80% (-)	98.12% (4.2)	98.68% (5)
5	98.24% (5)	97.51% (-)	98.18% (4.6)	98.83% (5)
6	–	98.10% (9)	98.18% (4.3)	98.83% (5)
7	–	97.95% (8)	98.25% (4.7)	98.98% (5)

[a] Data extracted from Tables 2.4 and 2.5

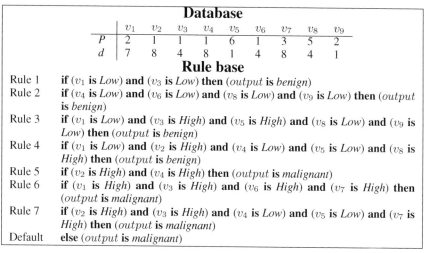

Database

	v_1	v_2	v_3	v_4	v_5	v_6	v_7	v_8	v_9
P	2	1	1	1	6	1	3	5	2
d	7	8	4	8	1	4	8	4	1

Rule base

Rule 1   **if** (v_1 **is** *Low*) **and** (v_3 **is** *Low*) **then** (*output* **is** *benign*)

Rule 2   **if** (v_4 **is** *Low*) **and** (v_6 **is** *Low*) **and** (v_8 **is** *Low*) **and** (v_9 **is** *Low*) **then** (*output* **is** *benign*)

Rule 3   **if** (v_1 **is** *Low*) **and** (v_3 **is** *High*) **and** (v_5 **is** *High*) **and** (v_8 **is** *Low*) **and** (v_9 **is** *Low*) **then** (*output* **is** *benign*)

Rule 4   **if** (v_1 **is** *Low*) **and** (v_2 **is** *High*) **and** (v_4 **is** *Low*) **and** (v_5 **is** *Low*) **and** (v_8 **is** *High*) **then** (*output* **is** *benign*)

Rule 5   **if** (v_2 **is** *High*) **and** (v_4 **is** *High*) **then** (*output* **is** *malignant*)

Rule 6   **if** (v_1 **is** *High*) **and** (v_3 **is** *High*) **and** (v_6 **is** *High*) **and** (v_7 **is** *High*) **then** (*output* **is** *malignant*)

Rule 7   **if** (v_2 **is** *High*) **and** (v_3 **is** *High*) **and** (v_4 **is** *Low*) **and** (v_5 **is** *Low*) **and** (v_7 **is** *High*) **then** (*output* **is** *malignant*)

Default   **else** (*output* **is** *malignant*)

Fig. 4.2. The best evolved, fuzzy diagnostic system with seven rules. It exhibits an overall classification rate of 98.98%, and its longest rule includes 5 variables.

Database

	v_1	v_2	v_3	v_4	v_5	v_6	v_7	v_8	v_9
P	3		1	3	4	5		7	2
d	8		3	1	2	2		4	1

Rule base

Rule 1   **if** (v_1 **is** *Low*) **and** (v_3 **is** *Low*) **and** (v_5 **is** *Low*) **then** (*output* **is** *benign*)

Rule 2   **if** (v_1 **is** *Low*) **and** (v_4 **is** *Low*) **and** (v_6 **is** *Low*) **and** (v_8 **is** *Low*) **and** (v_9 **is** *Low*) **then** (*output* **is** *benign*)

Default   **else** (*output* **is** *malignant*)

Fig. 4.3. The best evolved, fuzzy diagnostic system with two rules. It exhibits an overall classification rate of 98.54%, and a maximum of 5 variables in the longest rule.

I next describe two of my top-performance systems, which serve to exemplify the solutions found by Fuzzy CoCo. The first system, delineated in Figure 4.2, presents the highest classification performance evolved to date. It consists of seven rules with the longest rule including 5 variables. This system obtains an overall classification rate (i.e., over the entire database) of 98.98%.

In addition to the above seven-rule system, evolution found systems with between 2 and 6 rules exhibiting excellent classification performance, i.e., higher than 98.5% (Table 4.3). Among these systems, I consider as the most interesting the system with the smallest number of conditions (i.e., total number of variables in the rules). Figure 4.3 presents one such two-rule system, containing a total of 8 conditions, and which obtains an overall classification rate of 98.54%; its longest rule has 5 variables.

The improvement attained by Fuzzy CoCo, while seemingly slight (0.5-1%) is in fact quite significant. A 1% improvement implies 7 additional cases which are classified correctly. At the performance rates in question (above 98%) every additional case is hard-won. Indeed, try as I did with the fuzzy-genetic approach—tuning parameters and tweaking the setup—I arrived at a performance impasse. Fuzzy CoCo, however, readily churned out better-performance systems, which were able to classify a significant number of additional cases; moreover, these systems were evolved in less time.

Such improvement should also obey to an overfitting phenomenon. The only way to assess whether this hypothesis is correct or not would be a computationally-expensive generalization analysis. Nevertheless, a thorough generality analysis (see Section 5.4) shows that, for the best system found (i.e., the seven-rule system shown in Figure 4.2), all the rules but one are quite general.

4.2 Mammography Interpretation: The COBRA System

This section presents the design of a tool based on Fuzzy CoCo denominated "CO-BRA: Catalonia online breast-cancer risk assessor." COBRA is designed to aid radiologists in the interpretation of mammography to decide whether to perform a biopsy on a patient or not. Mammography remains the principal technique for detecting breast cancer. Despite its undoubtable value in reducing mortality, mammography's positive predictive value (PPV) is low: only between 15 and 35% of mammographic-detected lesions are cancerous [71, 84]. The remaining 65 to 85% of biopsies, besides being costly and time-consuming, cause understandable stress on women facing the shadow of cancer. A computer-based tool that assists radiologists during mammographic interpretation would contribute to increasing the PPV of biopsy recommendations.

4.2.1 The Catalonia Mammography Database

The *Catalonia mammography database*, which is the object of this section, was collected at the Duran y Reynals hospital in Barcelona. It consists of 15 input attributes and a diagnostic result indicating whether or not a carcinoma was detected after a biopsy. The 15 input attributes include three clinical characteristics (Table 4.4) and two groups of six radiologic features, according to the type of lesion found in the mammography: mass or microcalcifications (Table 4.5).

A radiologist fills out a reading form for each mammography, assigning values for the clinical characteristics and for one of the groups of radiologic features. Then, the radiologist interprets the case using a five-point scale: (1) benign; (2) probably benign; (3) indeterminate; (4) probably malignant; (5) malignant. According to this interpretation a decision is made on whether to practice a biopsy on the patient or not. The Catalonia database contains data corresponding to 227 cases, all of them sufficiently suspect to justify a biopsy recommendation. For the purpose of this study, each case was further examined by three different readers—for a total of

Table 4.4. Variables corresponding to a patient's clinical data.

v_1	Age		[28-82] years
v_2	Menstrual history	1	Premenopausal
		2	Postmenopausal
v_3	Family history	1	None
		2	Second familiar
		3	First familiar
		4	Contralateral
		5	Homolateral

Table 4.5. Variables corresponding to radiologic features. There are two groups of variables that describe the mammographic existence of microcalcifications and masses.

Microcalcifications	Mass

v_4 Disposition
  1 Round
  2 Indefinite
  3 Triangular or Trapezoidal
  4 Linear or Ramified
	v_{10} Morphology
	  1 Oval
	  2 Round
	  3 Lobulated
	  4 Polilobulated
	  5 Irregular

v_5 Other signs of group form
  1 None
  2 Major axis in direction of nip-
  3 Undulating contour ple
  4 Both previous
	v_{11} Margins
	  1 Well delimited
	  2 Partially well delimited
	  3 Poorly delimited
	  4 Spiculated

v_6 Maximum diameter of group
  [3-120] mm
	v_{12} Density greater than parenchyma
	  1 Not
	  2 Yes

v_7 Number
  1 <10
  2 10 to 30
  3 >30
	v_{13} Focal distortion
	  1 Not
	  2 Yes

v_8 Morphology
  1 Ring shaped
  2 Regular sharp-pointed
  3 Too small to determine
  4 Irregular sharp-pointed
  5 Vermicular, ramified
	v_{14} Focal asymmetry
	  1 Not
	  2 Yes

v_9 Size irregularity
  1 Very regular
  2 Sparingly regular
  3 Very irregular
	v_{15} Maximum diameter
	  [5-80] mm

681 readings—but only diverging readings were kept. The actual number of readings in the database is 516, among which 187 are positive (malignant) cases and 329 are negative (benign) cases.

4.2.2 Proposed Solution: The COBRA System

The solution scheme I propose, the so-called COBRA system, is depicted in Figure 4.4. It is composed of four elements: a user interface, a reading form, a database, and a diagnostic decision unit which is the core of the system. This latter consists of a fuzzy system and a threshold unit. Based on the 15 input attributes collected with the reading form, the fuzzy system computes a continuous appraisal value of the malignancy of a case. The threshold unit then outputs a biopsy recommendation according to the fuzzy system's output. The threshold value used in this system is 3, which corresponds to the "indeterminate" diagnostic. Fuzzy CoCo is applied to design the fuzzy system in charge of appraising malignancy [79, 80].

The web-based user interface was developed to provide online access to the system. In the developed tool, the user fills the reading form (see a snapshot in Figure 4.5). The COBRA provides, in addition to the final biopsy recommendation, information about the appraisal value computed by the fuzzy subsystem and about the rules involved in the decision (Figure 4.6 shows a snapshot of COBRA's output). The tool can be also used to train novel radiologists as the reading form can access previously diagnosed cases contained in the database. It is available at the URL: *http://lslwww.epfl.ch/~cobra.*

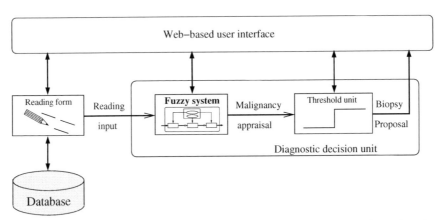

Fig. 4.4. The COBRA system comprises a user interface, a reading form—used to collect the patient's data from either the user or the database, a database containing selected cases, and a diagnostic decision unit which is the core of the system. In the decision unit the fuzzy system estimates the malignancy of the case and the threshold unit outputs a biopsy recommendation.

4.2.3 Fuzzy CoCo Setup

4.2.3.1 Fuzzy-Parameter Setup. I used prior knowledge about the Catalonia database to guide my choice of fuzzy parameters. In addition, I took into account the interpretability criteria presented in Section 2.3 to define constraints on the

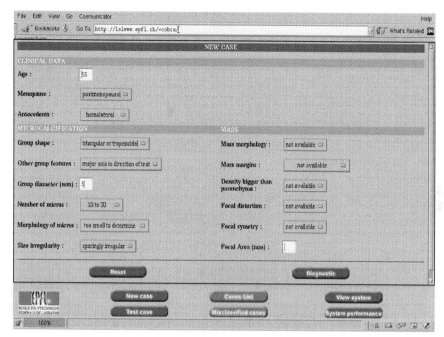

Fig. 4.5. User interface: reading form. The snapshot illustrates the reading form through which the COBRA system collects data about a case.

fuzzy parameters. Referring to Table 2.1, I delineate below the fuzzy system's set-up:

- Logical parameters: singleton-type fuzzy systems; min-max fuzzy operators; orthogonal, trapezoidal input membership functions (see Figure 4.7); weighted-average defuzzification.
- Structural parameters: two input membership functions (*Low* and *High*; see Figure 4.7); two output singletons (*benign* and *malignant*); a user-configurable number of rules. The relevant variables are one of Fuzzy CoCo's evolutionary objectives. *Low* and *High* linguistic labels may be further replaced by labels having medical meaning according to the specific context of each variable.
- Connective parameters: the antecedents and the consequent of the rules are searched by Fuzzy CoCo. The algorithm also searches for the consequent of the default rule. All rules have unitary weight.
- Operational parameters: the input membership-function values are to be found by Fuzzy CoCo. The values of P_1 and P_2 are restricted to the universe of each variable. For the output singletons I used the values 1 and 5, for *benign* and *malignant*, respectively.

4.2.3.2 Genome Encodings. Fuzzy CoCo thus searches for four parameters: input membership-function values, relevant input variables, and antecedents and consequents of rules. To encode these parameters into both species' genomes, which

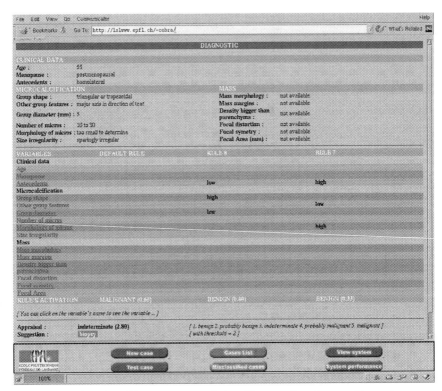

Fig. 4.6. User interface: biopsy recommendation. The snapshot shows a diagnostic recommendation for a given patient. Note that besides recommending to practice a biopsy, COBRA gives information about the appraisal value (indeterminate, 2.8), about the rules involved in the decision (rules 7, 8, and default), and about their truth value (0.33, 0.4, and 0.6, respectively).

together describe an entire fuzzy system, it is necessary to take into account the heterogeneity of the input variables as explained below.

- Species 1: Membership functions. The fifteen input variables ($v_1 - v_{15}$) present three different types of values: continuous ($v_1, v_6,$ and v_{15}), discrete ($v_3 - v_5$ and $v_7 - v_{11}$), and binary (v_2 and $v_{12} - v_{14}$). It is not necessary to encode membership functions for binary variables as they can only take on two values. The membership-function genome encodes the remaining 11 variables—three continuous and eight discrete—each with two parameters P_1 and P_2, defining the membership-function apices (Figure 4.7). Table 4.6 delineates the parameters encoding the membership-function genome.
- Species 2: Rules. The i-th rule has the form:
    if (v_1 is A_1^i) and ... and (v_{15} is A_{15}^i) then (*output* is C^i),
  where A_j^i can take on the values: 1 (*Low*), 2 (*High*), or 0 or 3 (*Don't care*). C^i can take on the values: 1 (*benign*) or 2 (*malignant*). As mentioned before, each

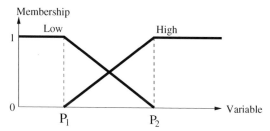

Fig. 4.7. Input fuzzy variables. Each fuzzy variable has two possible fuzzy values labeled **Low** and **High**, and orthogonal membership functions, plotted above as degree of membership versus input value. P_1 and P_2 define the membership-function apices.

Table 4.6. Genome encoding for membership-function species. Genome length is 106 bits.

Variable type	Qty	Parameters	Bits	Total bits
Continuous	3	2	7	42
Discrete	8	2	4	64
		Total Genome Length		106

database case presents three clinical characteristics and six radiologic features according to the type of lesion found: mass or microcalcifications (note that only a few special cases contain data for both groups). To take advantage of this fact, the rule-base genome encodes, for each rule, 11 parameters: the three antecedents of the clinical-data variables, the six antecedents of one radiological-feature group, an extra bit to indicate whether the rule applies for mass or microcalcifications, and the rule consequent. Furthermore, the genome contains an additional parameter corresponding to the consequent of the default rule. Relevant variables are searched for implicitly by allowing the algorithm to choose *Don't care* labels as valid antecedents ($A^i_j = 0$ or $A^i_j = 3$); in such a case the respective variable is considered irrelevant, and removed from the rule. Table 4.7 delineates the parameters encoding the rules genome.

Table 4.7. Genome encoding for rules species. Genome length is $(20 \times N_r) + 1$ bits, where N_r denotes the number of rules.

Parameters	Qty	Bits	Total bits
Clinical antecedents	$3 \times N_r$	2	$6 \times N_r$
Radiologic antecedents	$6 \times N_r$	2	$12 \times N_r$
Rule-type selector	N_r	1	N_r
Consequents	$N_r + 1$	1	$N_r + 1$
	Total Genome Length		$(20 \times N_r) + 1$

4.2.3.3 Evolutionary Parameters. Table 4.8 delineates values and ranges of values of the evolutionary parameters. The algorithm terminates when the maximum number of generations, G_{max}, is reached (I set $G_{max} = 700 + 200 \times N_r$, i.e., dependent on the number of rules used in the run), or when the increase in fitness of the best individual over five successive generations falls below a certain threshold (10^{-4} in these experiments).

Table 4.8. Fuzzy CoCo set-up for the COBRA system.

Parameter	Values
Population size N_p	90
Maximum generations G_{max}	$700 + 200N_r$
Crossover probability P_c	1
Mutation probability P_m	$\{0.005, 0.01\}$
Elitism rate E_r	$\{0.1, 0.2\}$
"Fit" cooperators N_{cf}	1
Random cooperators N_{cr}	1

4.2.3.4 Fitness Function. The fitness definition takes into account medical diagnostic criteria. The most commonly employed measures of the validity of diagnostic procedures are the sensitivity and specificity, the likelihood ratios, the predictive values, and the overall classification (accuracy) [9]. Table 4.9 provides expressions for four of these measures which are important for evaluating the performance of my systems. Three of them are used in the fitness function, the last one is used in Section 4.2.4 to support the analysis of the results. Besides these criteria, the fitness function provides extra selective pressure based on two syntactic criteria: simplicity and readability (see Section 2.3).

Table 4.9. Diagnostic performance measures. The values used to compute the expressions are: True positive (TP): the number of positive cases correctly detected, true negative (TN): the number of negative cases correctly detected, false positive (FP): the number of negative cases diagnosed as positive, and false negative (FN): the number of positive cases diagnosed as negative.

Sensitivity	$\dfrac{TP}{TP + FN}$
Specificity	$\dfrac{TN}{TN + FP}$
Accuracy	$\dfrac{TP + TN}{TP + TN + FP + FN}$
Positive predictive value (PPV)	$\dfrac{TP}{TP + FP}$

The fitness function combines the following five criteria: 1) F_{sens}: sensitivity, or true-positive ratio, computed as the percentage of positive cases correctly classified; 2) F_{spec}: specificity, or true-negative ratio, computed as the percentage of negative cases correctly classified (note that there is usually an important trade-off between sensitivity and specificity which renders difficult the satisfaction of both criteria); 3) F_{acc}: classification performance, computed as the percentage of cases correctly classified; 4) F_r: rule-base size fitness, computed as the percentage of unused rules (i.e., the number of rules that are never fired and can thus be removed altogether from the system); and 5) F_v: rule-length fitness, computed as the average percentage of *don't-care* antecedents—i.e., unused variables—per rule. This order also represents their relative importance in the final fitness function, from most important (F_{sens}) to least important (F_r and F_v).

The fitness function is computed in three steps—basic fitness, accuracy reinforcement, and size reduction—as explained below:

1. Basic fitness. Based on sensitivity and specificity, it is given by
$$F_1 = \frac{F_{sens} + \alpha F_{spec}}{1 + \alpha},$$

   where the weight factor $\alpha = 0.3$ reflects the greater importance of sensitivity.
2. Accuracy reinforcement. Given by
$$F_2 = \frac{F_1 + \beta F'_{acc}}{1 + \beta},$$

   where $\beta = 0.01$. $F'_{acc} = F_{acc}$ when $F_{acc} > 0.7$; $F'_{acc} = 0$ elsewhere. This step slightly reinforces the fitness of high-accuracy systems.
3. Size reduction. Based on the size of the fuzzy system, it is given by
$$F = \frac{F_2 + \gamma F_{size}}{1 + 2\gamma},$$

   where $\gamma = 0.01$. $F_{size} = (F_r + F_v)$ if $F_{acc} > 0.7$ and $F_{sens} > 0.98$; $F_{size} = 0$ elsewhere. This step rewards top systems exhibiting a concise rule set, thus directing evolution toward more interpretable systems.

4.2.4 Results

Two series of experiments were performed: (1) a first, limited series intended to estimate both attainable performance values and an adequate size of the rule base (i.e., where the systems evolved attain high performance levels); and (2) a more exhaustive series where Fuzzy CoCo was set to search for systems of a single, selected, rule-base size. Besides their central goal of searching for high-performance systems, in both series of experiments I included mechanisms to assess the generalization capabilities of Fuzzy CoCo for this problem.

4.2.4.1 First Series: Rule-Base Size Exploration. As mentioned before, the main goal of this series was to explore the potential performance of systems with different number of rules in their rule base. A total of 65 evolutionary runs were performed, all of which found systems whose fitness exceeds 0.83. In particular, considering the best individual per run (i.e., the evolved system with the highest fitness value), 42 runs led to a fuzzy system whose fitness exceeds 0.88, and of these, 6 runs found systems whose fitness exceeds 0.9. Table 4.10 shows the results of the best systems

Table 4.10. Results of the best systems evolved. Results are divided into four classes, in accordance with the maximum number of rules-per-system, going from 10-rule systems to 25-rule ones. Shown below are the fitness values of the top systems as well as the average fitness per class, along with the number of rules which effectively used by the system (R_{eff}) and the average number of variables per rule (V_r). The performance of the highlighted systems is presented in more detail in Table 4.11.

Maximum number	Best individual			Average per class		
of rules	Fitness	R_{eff}	V_r	Fitness	R_{eff}	V_r
10	**0.8910**	**9**	**2.22**	0.8754	9.17	2.52
15	0.8978	12	2.50	0.8786	12.03	2.62
20	0.9109	17	2.41	0.8934	14.15	2.59
25	**0.9154**	**17**	**2.70**	0.8947	15.78	2.76

obtained. The maximum number of rules per system was fixed at the outset to be between ten and twenty-five.

As mentioned before, the fitness function includes two syntactic criteria to favor the evolution of good diagnostic systems exhibiting interpretable rule bases (see Section 2.3). Concerning the simplicity of the rule base, rules that are encoded in a genotype but that never fire are removed from the phenotype (the final system), rendering it more interpretable. Moreover, to improve readability, the rules are allowed (and encouraged) to contain *don't-care* conditions. The relatively low values of R_{eff} and V_r in Table 4.10 confirm the reinforced interpretability of the evolved systems.

Table 4.11 shows the diagnostic performance of two selected evolved systems. The first system, which is the top one over all 65 Fuzzy CoCo runs, is a 17-rule system exhibiting a sensitivity of 99.47% (i.e., it detects all but one of the positive cases), and a specificity of 68.69% (i.e., 226 of the 329 negative cases are correctly detected as benign). The second system is the best found when searching for ten-rule systems. The sensitivity and the specificity of this 9-rule system are, respectively, 98.40% and 64.13%. As mentioned before, the usual positive predictive value (PPV) of mammography ranges between 15 and 35%. As shown in Table 4.11, Fuzzy CoCo increases this value beyond 60%—64.36% for the 17-rule system—while still exhibiting a very high sensitivity.

Table 4.11. Diagnostic performance of two selected evolved systems. Shown below are the sensitivity, the specificity, the accuracy, and the positive predictive value (PPV) of two selected systems (see Table 4.9). In parentheses are the values, expressed in number of cases, leading to such performance measures. The 17-rule system is the top system. The 9-rule system is the best found when searching for ten-rule systems.

	17-rule	9-rule
Sensitivity	99.47% (186/187)	98.40% (184/187)
Specificity	68.69% (226/329)	64.13% (211/329)
Accuracy	79.84% (412/516)	76.55% (395/516)
PPV	64.36% (186/289)	60.93% (184/302)

Additional to this series of experiments, I applied ten-fold cross validation [116] in order to (coarsely) assess the generalization capabilities of the fuzzy systems obtained. For each ten-fold test the data set is first partitioned into ten equal-sized sets, then each set is in turn used as the test set while Fuzzy CoCo trains on the other nine sets. Table 4.12 presents the average results obtained performing six cross-validation runs for several rule-base sizes. The percent difference between training and test sets is relatively low, even for large rule bases, suggesting low overfitting.

Table 4.12. Results of ten-fold cross-validation. Results are divided into six classes, going from 3-rule systems to 30-rule ones. Shown below is the average fitness per class obtained in both training and test sets (the fitness represents the average of the average fitnesses for the six cross-validation runs), along with the difference between training and test performances, expressed both in absolute value and percentage.

Maximum number of rules	Training set	Test set	Difference	Percentage
3	0.8269	0.7865	0.0404	4.89
7	0.8511	0.8036	0.0474	5.58
10	0.8712	0.8030	0.0682	7.83
15	0.8791	0.8125	0.0666	7.58
20	0.8814	0.8244	0.0569	6.47
30	0.8867	0.8104	0.0763	8.60

Note that, because of the relatively reduced size of the Catalonia database, a deeper generalization analysis should require a computationally-expensive strategy like leave-one-out [116]. Performing such analysis on all the tested rule-base sizes becomes prohibitive because of the huge number of required runs. Instead, I took advantage of the second series—presented below—to finely evaluate the generalization capabilities of Fuzzy CoCo for the Catalonia mammography database.

4.2.4.2 Second Series: 20-Rule Systems. The results obtained in the first series of experiments (Table 4.10) show that the best systems found, which effectively use 17 rules, were found searching for 20- and 25-rule systems. Based on this, I chose to search, more exhaustively, for fuzzy systems with up to 20 rules in order to explore a promising region of the search space. A total of 469 evolutionary runs were performed. Table 4.13 shows the diagnostic performance of both the average and the best run of all evolutionary runs as well as those of the leave-5-out cross validation, which are analyzed below. Note that the positive predictive value (PPV) is still high: 58.32% for the average system and 64.93% for the best one as shown in Table 4.13.

The best evolved system exhibits a sensitivity of 100% and a specificity of 69.3% (i.e., 228 of the 329 negative cases are correctly detected as benign). Even though evolution was allowed to search for systems with 20 fuzzy rules, the best system found effectively uses 14 rules. In average, these rules contain 2.71 variables (out of 15) which are, furthermore, Boolean. Note that this latter fact does not contradict the use of a fuzzy approach as Boolean systems are a subset of the, more general,

Table 4.13. Diagnostic performance and leave-5-out cross validation. Shown below are the diagnostic performance values of the top and the average evolved systems together with those obtained on the test-set. In parentheses are the number of cases, leading to each measure.

Performance measure	Best system	Average	Average test
Fitness	0.9166	0.8834	0.8566
Sensitivity	100% (187/187)	98.78% (184.7/187)	95.72% (179/187)
Specificity	69.30% (228/329)	59.69% (196.4/329)	60.18% (198/329)
Accuracy	80.43% (415/516)	73.86% (381.1/516)	73.06% (377/516)
PPV	64.93% (187/288)	58.32% (184.7/316.7)	57.74% (179/310)

set of fuzzy systems. In fact, while fuzzy modeling techniques may find Boolean solutions, the contrary does not hold.

This series of experiments was conceived with the additional goal of finely evaluate the generalization capabilities of Fuzzy CoCo for the problem at hand. I performed four generalization tests using leave-5-out cross validation (which corresponds, for this problem to 103-fold cross-validation). For each test, the data set is partitioned into subsets (folds) of 5 instances each one. At each evolutionary run, a different fold is left out to serve as test set while Fuzzy CoCo trains on the remaining data. The test diagnostic performance is computed, according to the expressions presented in Table 4.9, cumulating the diagnostic figures (i.e., TP, TN, FP, and FN) through all the folds. As observed in Table 4.13, the test diagnostic performance is very good as compared with the best system found.

To illustrate how COBRA makes a diagnostic decision and the type of rules involved in it, we present four interesting example cases., as presented in Table 4.14. Cases 1 to 3 correspond to usual readings exhibiting either microcalcification or mass as radiologic features. Case 4 contains both types of features.

Table 4.14. Four examples of possible input readings.

Variable	Case 1	Case 2	Case 3	Case 4
		Clinical data		
Age	45	50	41	47
Menopause	pre	post	pre	pre
Antecedents	none	none	none	homolateral
		Microcalcifications		
Group shape	undefined	–	–	undefined
Other features	nipple-oriented	–	–	none
Diameter	12 mm	–	–	8 mm
Number	< 10	–	–	< 10
Morphology	Sharp-pointed	–	–	ring-shaped
Regularity	Spar. irregular	–	–	very regular
		Mass		
Morphology	–	round	oval	round
Margins	–	poorly delim.	poorly delim.	poorly delim.
Density	–	smaller	smaller	bigger
Distortion	–	no	yes	yes
Asymmetry	–	no	yes	no
Area	–	12 mm	10 mm	14 mm

For each case, the system evaluates the activation of each rule and takes into account the values of the proposed diagnostics—i.e., 1 for Benign and 5 for Malignant. The system's malignancy appraisal is computed as the weighted average of these diagnostics. The final biopsy is given to the user together with the rules participating in the decision. Table 4.15 shows the rules activated for each case, the diagnostic they propose, the appraisal value, and the final biopsy suggestion using 3 (i.e., indeterminate) as threshold.

Table 4.15. Rule activation, appraisal, and diagnostic suggestion for the four example cases.

Active rule	Case 1	Case 2	Case 3	Case 4
Rule 1	Benign	–	–	Benign
Rule 2	–	–	–	Benign
Rule 7	Benign	–	–	–
Rule 9	–	–	Benign	–
Rule 13	–	Malignant	–	Malignant
Rule 14	–	Malignant	Malignant	–
Appraisal	1 (Benign)	5 (Malignant)	3 (Indeterminate)	2.33 (Prob. Benign)
Suggestion	No biopsy	Biopsy	Biopsy	No biopsy

The system takes into account all active rules to compute a malignancy appraisal, that is it searches for, and ponders, all possible indicia of benignity and malignancy before making a decision. In particular, cases 3 and 4 illustrate well such behavior.

In summary, Fuzzy CoCo was able to evolve high-performance systems for two hard problems, with all systems exhibiting high interpretability.

5 Analyzing Fuzzy CoCo

In this book I proposed a novel coevolutionary approach to fuzzy modeling—Fuzzy CoCo—which I then applied to the solution of several hard problems. The experience acquired while exploring the usage and limitations of the method have permitted the extraction of guiding criteria to facilitate the use of Fuzzy CoCo. It is necessary, however, to perform further analysis to better understand the effect that some of the Fuzzy-CoCo parameters may have on its performance. It is also convenient to take a second look at the results obtained, in order to verify the consistency and the generality of the systems designed with Fuzzy CoCo.

This chapter is organized as follows: The next section presents a guide to applying Fuzzy CoCo. Section 5.2, after analyzing the effect of parameters on the performance of Fuzzy CoCo, proposes some qualitative relationships that may facilitate setting up the algorithm. Next, in Section 5.3, I discuss the consistency and the quality of the results obtained by Fuzzy CoCo for the different problems presented. Section 5.4 presents the concept of local generality and analyzes this aspect of the best systems found by Fuzzy CoCo. Finally, I summarize the chapter in Section 5.5.

5.1 A Stepwise Guide to Applying Fuzzy CoCo

Applying Fuzzy CoCo requires the definition of parameters of its two main components: (1) the fuzzy system and (2) the cooperative coevolutionary algorithm.

1. **Fuzzy-system parameters.** In Section 2.1 I classified the parameters of a fuzzy system into four categories: logical, structural, connective, and operational. Based on this classification, the following four-level procedure serves to define the fuzzy-system parameters:

    a) Define the logical parameters. As noted in Section 2.1, logical parameters are predefined by the designer based on experience and on problem characteristics. The user must define the type of fuzzy system (e.g., singleton-type), the operators used for AND, OR, implication, and aggregation operations (e.g., min-max operators), the type of membership functions (e.g., orthogonal, trapezoidal ones), and the defuzzyfication method (e.g., COA).

C.A. Peña Reyes: Coevolutionary Fuzzy Modeling, LNCS 3204, pp. 89-102, 2004.
© Springer-Verlag Berlin Heidelberg 2004

b) Choose the structural parameters.
  – A set of relevant variables should be defined. Usually, this set includes *all* the available variables, as Fuzzy CoCo can be set to automatically reduce their number.
  – Fuzzy CoCo requires predefining the number of membership functions. Although this number could be set to a relatively high value to then let Fuzzy CoCo seek automatically an efficient subset of the membership functions, this strategy must be used carefully. The increase in the size of the search space may prevent Fuzzy CoCo from converging towards good results.
  – The number of rules is fixed (by the designer) for a given Fuzzy-CoCo run. A discussion about this number is presented in Section 5.2.1.
c) Encode the connective parameters into the rules genome. The rules may be either complete (i.e., containing at least one antecedent for each variable) or incomplete (i.e., using *don't-care* labels). The antecedents in rules may be connected merely by the AND operator, or may contain also OR and NOT operators. Fuzzy CoCo thus offers the designer the freedom of choosing any type of rule, given that there exists a proper way to encode it. If the problem requires a good interpretability, the syntactic criteria presented in Section 2.3 must be taken into account to constrain the definition of the rules genome.
d) Encode the operational parameters into the membership-function genome. The membership functions can be of arbitrary form. The only condition imposed by Fuzzy CoCo is that all possible labels implied by the rules species should be defined. Besides, to reinforce the interpretability of the system, the semantic criteria presented in Section 2.3 should be used to define some restrictions on the definition of the membership functions.

Note that Fuzzy CoCo is a methodology for improving the performance and speed of the fuzzy-modeling process. It cannot correct on its own wrong decisions made during the definition of the fuzzy-system parameters. Thus, the designer need posses knowledge of the problem or a good evaluation heuristics.

2. **Coevolutionary parameters.** Once both genomes—rules and membership-functions—are encoded, the coevolutionary parameters presented below must be set according to a number of criteria, the two most important being computational costliness and exploration-exploitation tradeoff. A discussion concerning the qualitative relations among the ranges of the coevolutionary parameters is presented in Section 5.2.6.
  a) Population size $\|P_S\|$. Fuzzy CoCo requires smaller populations than a simple genetic algorithm; typically, 50 to 80 percent smaller. This markedly reduces the computational cost. In the WBCD example, typical population sizes in Fuzzy CoCo are 40 to 80, while the standard fuzzy-genetic approach uses 200 individuals. A deeper analysis of the effects of $\|P_S\|$ is presented in Section 5.2.2.

b) Number of cooperators N_c. Typical values range from 1 to 6 (1 to 3 "fit" cooperators and 0 to 4 random cooperators). The number of "fit" cooperators N_{cf} directly affects exploitation, while the number of random cooperators N_{cr} directly affects exploration. Both of them affect the computational cost. The effects of this parameter are analyzed in Section 5.2.3.

c) Crossover probability P_c. There is no special consideration concerning the value of P_c in Fuzzy CoCo. Standard values—0.5 to 1—are used [61].

d) Mutation probability P_m. As discussed in Section 3.3, due to an exploration-exploitation tradeoff with the elitism rate, P_m values in Fuzzy CoCo are usually an order of magnitude higher than in a simple genetic algorithm. While the value of P_m proposed by Potter and De Jong ($P_m = 1/L_g$ where $L_g = length(genome)$) [88] can be applied with relatively large populations, it has to be increased by up to 10 times when Fuzzy CoCo is applied with small populations. See Section 5.2.4 for an analysis of the effects of P_m on Fuzzy CoCo performance.

e) Elitism Rate E_r. Typical values for E_r are between 0.1 and 0.4, where larger values are required in systems with few rules and small populations. E_r encourages exploitation of solutions found. Section 5.2.5 analyzes the effects of this parameter on the performance of Fuzzy CoCo.

f) Maximum number of generations G_{max}. Due to the speed gain offered by Fuzzy CoCo, the value G_{max}, related directly to computational cost, can be up to five times smaller than single-population algorithms. For example, for a 5-rule system in the WBCD problem, while Fuzzy CoCo runs 1500 generations, the fuzzy-genetic approach runs 4500 generations.

5.2 Effects of Some Parameters on Performance

Fuzzy CoCo requires the designer to define a number of interdependent parameters that affect directly or indirectly the performance of the algorithm. In this section I analyze the effects that five of these parameters have on the algorithm's performance and on its dynamics—i.e., the way in which this performance evolves. The five parameters analyzed are: number of rules, population size, number of cooperators, mutation probability, and elitism rate.

For the purpose of this analysis, I use a simple *ad hoc* experiment based on the WBCD problem (Section 4.1). The experiment consists of 125 Fuzzy-CoCo runs in which the sole criterion maximized is the classification performance (i.e., the fitness function does not include any interpretability criteria). In order to investigate the effect of each parameter, Fuzzy CoCo is tested with five different values of the concerned parameter. The fitness reported in each case is the average of five runs.

Table 5.1 shows the values used in this experiment. Note that as some of these parameters may affect the number of fuzzy systems evaluated per generation, I used the cumulative number of fitness evaluations instead of the number of generations, to represent the computational effort. Consequently, the parameter G_{max} (maximum

number of generations) is substituted by the maximum number of fitness evaluations F_{max}. This value, set to 4×10^5, is lower than those used by Fuzzy CoCo in
Section 4.1, as this analysis does not intend to find better systems than those already
obtained.

Table 5.1. Fuzzy CoCo set-up for the WBCD problem used to analyze the effects of some
parameters.

Parameter	Default value	Tested values
Number of rules N_r	5	$\{2, 3, 5, 8, 12\}$
Population size $\|P_S\|$	70	$\{20, 30, 50, 80, 120\}$
Crossover probability P_c	1	—
Mutation probability P_m	0.05	$\{0.001, 0.005, 0.01, 0.05, 0.1\}$
Elitism rate E_r	0.1	$\{0.03, 0.1, 0.2, 0.4, 0.6\}$
"Fit" cooperators N_{cf}	1	—
Random cooperators N_{cr}	1	$\{0, 1, 2, 3, 4\}$
Maximum fitness evaluations F_{max}	4×10^5	—

The first parameter analyzed—number of rules—principally affects the size and
the shape of the search space. The next two parameters, population size and number
of cooperators, define the number of fuzzy systems evaluated per generation. Then,
I analyze the effects of mutation probability and elitism rate. Finally, I derive some
qualitative relationships between these parameters.

5.2.1 Number of Rules

Figures 5.1 (a) and (b) show the evolution of Fuzzy CoCo performance for different numbers of rules. One can observe that, even though larger systems evolve
faster initially, at about 5000 fitness evaluations all the systems exhibit similar performance. From that point onward larger systems continue to increase their fitness
while smaller ones tend to stagnate (Figure 5.1.b). Note that 12-rule systems evolve
slowly and perform worst than slightly smaller ones.

For a given problem, searching for a compact fuzzy rule base is harder than
searching for a slightly larger system, even if the genome is larger for this latter search. The reason for this apparent contradiction is that a less compact fuzzy
system—i.e., with more rules—can cover a larger part of the problem space.
However, if evolution seeks too many rules, the fitness landscape becomes too
"flat" (intuitively, an abundance of low-performance hills, rather than a few high-
performance mountains), thus rendering the search more difficult. This idea is reinforced by the systems found for the COBRA problem (Table 4.10), which effectively
utilize between 63% and 91% of the number of rules encoded into the genome (respectively, 15.78 rules for 25-rule runs and 9.13 for 10-rule runs). It seems clear that
for each problem there exists a range of ideal rule-base sizes (between 4 and 7 for
the WBCD problem, and about 17 for the COBRA system). Besides trial and error,
I am aware of no current method to determine this range.

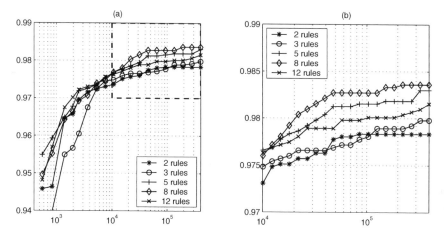

Fig. 5.1. Evolution of fitness as a function of the maximum number of rules. The figures show the average fitness of Fuzzy CoCo runs for different values of N_r. The inset box in (a)—corresponding to a steadier evolution of the fitness—is enlarged in (b). The abscissa represents the computational effort measured in number of fitness evaluations.

5.2.2 Population Size

As mentioned before, coevolutionary algorithms involve smaller populations than single-population algorithms. One clear advantage of such smaller populations is the fast evaluation of each generation. However, under these conditions the population might not have enough individuals to perform both exploration of the search space and exploitation of good solutions. Consequently, the search can stagnate after a limited number of generations. Figure 5.2, which shows the evolution of the fitness for different population sizes, corroborates this surmise. Indeed, populations of 20 individuals evolve fast (around 3000 fitness evaluations) to fitness values close to their maximum, while larger populations take longer to reach such performance levels. Observation of the steadier evolution stage (Figure 5.2.b) shows that the largest population (i.e., 120 individuals) outperforms the group formed by medium-size populations (30, 50, and 80 individuals). 20-individual populations almost stagnate at this stage of evolution.

The above analysis suggests that when applying Fuzzy CoCo to a given problem the use of small populations would provide a fast, accurate estimate of attainable fitness values. This can be useful for coarse-tuning the fitness function and the genetic operators. Medium-size populations would then be used to fine-tune the algorithm. The final search should be performed using large populations in order to provide the algorithm with the diversity required to adequately explore the search space.

5.2.3 Number of Cooperators

As noted in Section 5.1, the number of selected fit and random cooperators (N_{cf} and N_{cr}), besides affecting the computational cost of the algorithm, are parameters

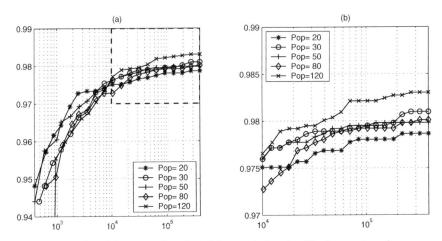

Fig. 5.2. Evolution of fitness as a function of the population size. The figures show the average fitness of Fuzzy CoCo runs for different values of $\|P_S\|$. The inset box of (a)—corresponding to a steadier evolution of the fitness—is enlarged in (b). The abscissa represents the computational effort measured in number of fitness evaluations.

related, respectively, to exploitation and exploration capabilities of Fuzzy CoCo. However, in contrast to elitism and mutation, these two parameters do not affect directly the genetic pool of the next generation, only affecting it indirectly by permitting Fuzzy CoCo to evaluate more accurately individual fitness. Figure 5.3 shows the evolution of fitness for different numbers of cooperators. As in the case of population size, systems with few fitness evaluations per generation (i.e., with one or two cooperators) evolve fast and provide solutions with "acceptable" fitness in approximately 5000 fitness evaluations. In the long term (i.e., more than 10^5 evaluations—see Figure 5.3.b) all the systems perform similarly. Only the systems using five cooperators perform slightly better.

Thus, concerning the number of cooperators, it seems that a light setup, with few cooperators, might be used in the earliest stages of the design of a solution based on Fuzzy CoCo. Once the fitness function has been adjusted the search can be performed using more cooperators. Note, however, that the present analysis did not evaluate the combined effect of simultaneously having a large population *and* a high number of cooperators, both of which are computationally costly strategies.

5.2.4 Mutation Probability

Figure 5.4 shows the effect that mutation probability has on the evolution of the fitness. The initial evolution (i.e., up to 20000 fitness evaluations) does not depend much on the mutation. In a later stage of evolution (Figure 5.4.b), moderate values of mutation probability—i.e., 0.005 and 0.01, corresponding approximately to $0.5/L_g$ and $1/L_g$, where L_g is the genome's length—seem to be the most adequate.

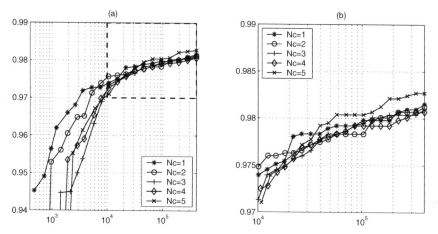

Fig. 5.3. Evolution of fitness as a function of the number of cooperators. The figures show the average fitness of Fuzzy CoCo runs for different values of $N_c = N_{cf} + N_{cr}$. The inset box of (a)—corresponding to a steadier evolution of the fitness—is enlarged in (b). The abscissa represents the computational effort measured in number of fitness evaluations.

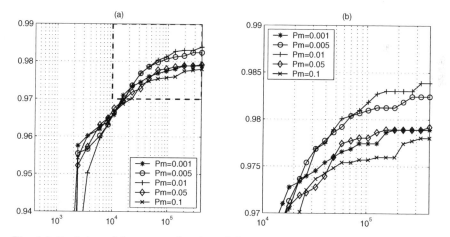

Fig. 5.4. Evolution of fitness as a function of the mutation probability. The figures show the average fitness of Fuzzy CoCo runs for different values of P_m. The inset box of (a)—corresponding to a steadier evolution of the fitness—is enlarged in (b). The abscissa represents the computational effort measured in number of fitness evaluations.

5.2.5 Elitism Rate

Observing the initial evolution of the fitness for different elitism rates (Figure 5.5.a) one can see that, during the first 10000 evaluations, Fuzzy CoCo runs using an elitism rate of 10% perform better, while runs with an elitism rate of 3% (corresponding to an elite with 2 individuals) perform significantly worse. This latter trend is confirmed in the long term (Figure 5.5.a), whereas the use of an elitism rate of 40% appears as a slightly better alternative than the others.

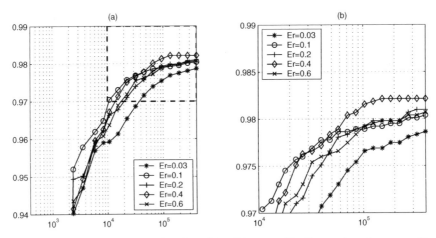

Fig. 5.5. Evolution of fitness as a function of the elitism rate. The figures show the average fitness of Fuzzy CoCo runs for different values of E_r. The inset box of (a)—corresponding to a steadier evolution of the fitness—is enlarged in (b). The abscissa represents the computational effort measured in number of fitness evaluations.

5.2.6 Qualitative Relationships

The analysis presented above describes the effects that some parameters have on the performance of Fuzzy CoCo for a given problem. However, these effects are evaluated by modifying, each time, only the involved parameter. Many more tests would be necessary to assess the combined effects of two or more parameters (e.g., to determine an adequate combination of values of P_m and E_r) in order to characterize completely the performance of the method. The same exhaustive analysis should be performed for different problems so as to identify whether or not these effects depend on the problem under study.

Instead of such an arduous analysis, I have derived some qualitative relationships between various parameters of Fuzzy CoCo. Shown in Table 5.2, these relationships are based on the simulations carried out on the different problems presented above.

5.3 Consistency and Quality of Results

Fuzzy CoCo has proven capable of finding good solutions to hard problems. Such good results emerge consistently as witnessed by the small differences observed between the best systems reported and the average results, as well as by

Table 5.2. Qualitative relationships between Fuzzy CoCo parameters. Delineated below are criteria to guide the choice of the number of cooperators N_c, the mutation probability P_m (expressed as a function of the genome's length, L_g), and the elitism rate E_r, all three as a function of the desired number of rules and of the desired population size (expressed in terms of percentage of the typical population size of a single-population algorithm). For example, if the user wishes to employ a large population with few rules then she should set N_c, P_m, and E_r to values within the ranges specified in the upper-right quadrant of the table.

Number of rules	Population size	
	Small (20%–40%)	Large (40%–70%)
Few (2–4)	N_c many (4–6) P_m large $((8-10)/L_g)$ E_r high (0.4–0.6)	some or many (3–6) medium $((4-6)/L_g)$ medium–high (0.3–0.6)
Many (4–10)	N_c few or some (2–5) P_m small or medium $((2-5)/L_g)$ E_r medium (0.2–0.4)	few (1–3) small $((1-2)/L_g)$ low (0.1–0.2)

the distribution of the results shown in the corresponding histograms (see sections 3.4.3, 4.1.2, 4.2.4). This fact is exemplified in Figure 5.6, showing the fitness evolution of the best, the worst, and the average runs of a given Fuzzy CoCo setup.

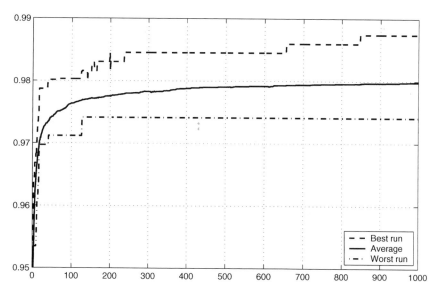

Fig. 5.6. Evolution of the best, the worst, and the average runs of a given Fuzzy CoCo setup. The curves correspond to 40 evolutionary runs, searching for 7-rule systems for the WBCD problem. The difference between the best and the worst runs is around 1%.

The consistency of the results does not provide information concerning the quality of the systems obtained by Fuzzy CoCo. This is usually done by comparing the results with previously published works. Because previous results for the Catalonia database are only partially available, I have opted for the use of a standard test that provides a rough estimation of the attainable performance: An intuitive, simple method known as *k-nearest-neighbor (knn)*.

The knn method [116] is a classification technique based on the memorization of a training database. Given an unclassified input case, the system searches the memory for the k training cases that most strongly resemble the new one. The resemblance is usually measured through a distance metric—e.g., Manhattan or Euclidean distances. The closest training cases are called the nearest neighbors. The unknown case is assigned the class of the majority of its k-nearest neighbors. Table 5.3 shows the performance obtained applying knn to the problems presented in this book and their comparison with the results obtained by Fuzzy CoCo.

Table 5.3. Comparison of Fuzzy CoCo with knn. Knn is used to roughly estimate an attainable fitness value. Shown below are the classification performance values obtained for each problem, along with the number of misclassifications in parentheses. The values for the COBRA system correspond to the basic fitness F_1 described in Section 4.2 that depends on sensitivity and specificity.

Problem	knn prediction	Fuzzy CoCo			
		Rules	Runs	Average	Best
Iris (controller)	0.9733 (4)	3	49	0.9910 (1.35)	1.0000 (0)
Iris (classifier)	0.9733 (4)	3	48	0.9751 (3.74)	0.9933 (1)
WBCD	0.9736 (18)	7	40	0.9825 (11.95)	0.9898 (7)
Cobra	0.7441	25	15	0.8947	0.9154

These comparisons allow to relativize the results obtained for a given problem. For the Iris and the WBCD problem, we can expect classification performances over 97.33%. However, this does not imply that slightly higher performance values can be easily attained, as they correspond to new correctly-classified cases that are hard to obtain, usually accepting increased complexity of the solution. On the other hand, fitness values obtained for the COBRA system, close to 0.89, while seemingly low in comparison with those of the WBCD problem, are in fact good results that correspond to an increase of more than 200 correctly-diagnosed cases with respect to knn results. Note that other machine-learning methods can be used to estimate the attainable fitness values.

5.4 Generality of the Designed Fuzzy Systems

The generalization capability of fuzzy systems is usually assessed at a global level through well-known generalization tests (e.g., k-fold cross-validation, as those presented for the Catalonia database in Section 4.2.4). However, little emphasis is put on the local generality of those fuzzy systems—i.e., the generality of their rules—although this latter may affect the global generalization capability. Indeed, overfitting in fuzzy systems is due to very specific rules that describe exceptional conditions instead of general patterns.

In this section I analyze local generality and the effect that some fuzzy parameters can have on it. I propose that the interpretability considerations presented in Section 2.3 may reinforce the local generality of fuzzy systems. I then analyze the generality of the fuzzy systems designed with Fuzzy CoCo to solve the Iris problem and the WBCD problem.

5.4.1 Generality of Fuzzy Rules

A fuzzy rule is said to be *general* with respect to a given input space, if it covers a significant portion of this space. Note that generality depends on the significance—in terms of information—of the region covered and not on its extension, although significance and extension are often related. When the input space is presented discretely, as is the case for the problems considered in this book, the generality of a rule is expressed in terms of the number of instances it covers. Given that this concept is related only with the input space, the generality of a rule does not imply its adequacy to describe a specific mapping between the input and the output spaces. Moreover, high performance is often attained at the expense of local generality. (Note that this measure may be skewed by ill-sampled training sets, where non-significant regions of the actual input space are over-represented.)

Even though generality is defined at the rule level, some parameters of the whole fuzzy system may affect its generality as discussed below:

– Membership functions per variable. The number of membership functions defining a linguistic variable, also known as granularity, influences the fineness of the partition and hence the capacity of the rules to target many reduced portions of the input space. In general, a reduced number of membership functions favors the existence of general rules.
– Variables per rule. Intuitively, the less variables in a rule's premise, the more extended may be the portion of the input space it covers. As explained in Section 2.3, several long rules are needed to cover the same space than a short rule does.
– Rules per system. The coverage that a fuzzy system can attain for a given input space, depends on the cumulative coverage of its rules. If the system disposes of only a few rules, in order to guarantee an adequate coverage these rules will tend to be general. Good performance requires good coverage. One can say that a small fuzzy system cannot do both: perform well and overlearn.

Note that generality is a meaningful concept both linguistically and numerically speaking. Because of this, the strategies proposed to reinforce the interpretability of fuzzy systems (Section 2.3.3) also favor the emergence of general rules. That is explained below:

– The use of common shared labels prevents each rule from defining its own membership functions. This avoids the existence of erratic rules tuned to very specific conditions.

– *Don't-care* conditions promote the existence of rules with few variables in their premise.
– The default rule is, by definition, a general rule. It provides coverage for wide (and sometimes disjoint) regions that would require many specific rules to describe them.

The example presented in Figure 5.7 illustrates how these strategies allow to improve the generality of the rule base while preserving classification performance. The rule in the center of the input space, albeit being specific in terms of extension, is quite general as it represents one third of the cases contained in the hypothetic database. The rule containing a *don't-care* condition, marked A covers the space of three more-specific rules. The default rule, marked D, covers the space of several very-specific rules including coverage for a region without any instance.

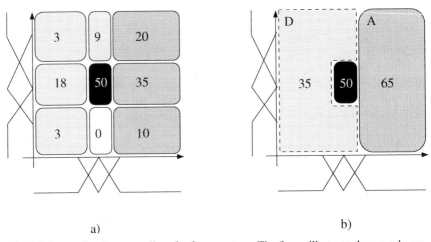

a)   b)

Fig. 5.7. Improving the generality of a fuzzy system. The figure illustrates how a rule containing a *don't-care* condition and a default rule (marked A and D, respectively) increase the generality of the system. The numbers in the rules represent the cases covered by the rule. The colors represent the output class proposed by each rule. Note that the classification performance of the system is preserved.

5.4.2 Generality of the Systems Designed by Fuzzy CoCo

To design the fuzzy systems presented throughout this book, I used Fuzzy CoCo to search for both high performance and high interpretability. Generality was not explicitly used as design-driving criterion. As mentioned before, the strategies used to favor interpretability may also result in the design of general rules. But if generality constitutes a priority when designing fuzzy systems for a given problem, the criteria presented herein must be used to constrain the representation of the fuzzy system, the fitness function, or both. Below I analyze the generality of the rules of the best systems presented in previous chapters.

5.4.2.1 The Three-Rule Fuzzy Controller for the Iris Problem. Recall that the best controller-type system that solves the Iris problem—presented in Figure 3.9— has three short rules (1.7 variables per rule). It classifies correctly all the cases in the database. Table 5.4 shows the activation figures of the three rules of this system, which serve to analyze their generality.

Table 5.4. Generality of the three-rule fuzzy controller. The activation profile of each rule consists of: number of firing instances, winning instances, instances where it fires alone, average activation level, and maximum activation. Note that the average activation level is computed using only the firing instances. The Iris database has 150 instances.

Rule	Number of instances			Firing level	
	fired	winner	alone	average	maximum
Rule 1	102	63	3	0.71	1
Rule 2	34	32	0	0.97	1
Rule 3	4	0	0	0.45	0.53
Default	115	61	48	0.63	1

Two of the active rules (i.e., rules 1 and 2) and the default rule are clearly general as they are involved in the classification of many instances. In contrast, rule 3 is more specific as it is fired only by 4 instances. However, despite its specificity, rule 3 never fires alone and it is never the winner rule. Note that the four instances for which rule 3 fires are hard to classify. Indeed, they lie close to the border between the classes *versicolor* and *virginica* in the input space.

5.4.2.2 The Three-Rule Fuzzy Classifier for the Iris Problem. The best classifier-type system found to solve the Iris problem, presented in Figure 3.11, has three short rules (2.3 variables per rule). It classifies correctly all but one instance in the database. The three rule-activation figures used to analyze the generality of the system are presented in Table 5.5.

Table 5.5. Generality of the three-rule fuzzy classifier. The activation profile of each rule consists of: number of firing instances, number of winning instances, number of instances where it fires alone, average activation level, and maximum activation. Note that the average activation level is computed using only the firing instances. The Iris database has 150 instances.

Rule	Number of instances			Firing level	
	fired	winner	alone	average	maximum
Rule 1	60	50	41	0.85	1
Rule 2	74	45	0	0.55	0.96
Rule 3	47	2	0	0.20	0.50
Default	109	53	32	0.54	1

It is clear from their firing profiles that all the rules are general. Even rule 3, whose premise is very specific—it defines conditions for all four input variables (see Figure 3.11)—fires for 47 instances.

5.4.2.3 The Seven-Rule System for the WBCD Problem. The best evolved system for the WBCD problem (see Figure 4.3) consists of 7 rules with an average of 3.4 variables per rule. This system classifies correctly 98.98% of the 683 instances in the WBCD database (i.e., it misclassifies 7 instances). Rule generality is analyzed through the activation figures presented in Table 5.6.

Table 5.6. Generality of the seven-rule WBCD fuzzy system. The activation profile of each rule consists of: number of firing instances, number of winning instances, number of instances where it fires alone, average activation level, and maximum activation. Note that the average activation level is computed using only the firing instances. The WBCD database has 683 instances.

Rule	Number of instances			Firing level	
	fired	winner	alone	average	maximum
Rule 1	482	202	8	0.74	1
Rule 2	438	386	1	0.91	1
Rule 3	12	3	0	0.43	0.75
Rule 4	52	2	0	0.22	0.63
Rule 5	239	106	2	0.47	1
Rule 6	183	48	0	0.39	0.88
Rule 7	115	21	0	0.29	0.75
Default	305	149	8	0.43	1

All but one of the active rules and the default rule are clearly general as they are involved in the classification of many instances. In contrast, rule 3 is more specific (it fires for only 12 instances) and relatively long (its premise contains 5 variables). However, despite its specificity, rule 3 never fires alone and it is the winner rule for only two instances.

5.5 Summary

In this chapter I presented some analyses that should guide future users of Fuzzy CoCo in their experimental design. First, I presented the steps required to define all the parameters of the algorithm. Secondly, I proposed some qualitative criteria to define the values of the most important parameters, based on an analysis of their effect on Fuzzy CoCo performance. Then, to analyze the quality of the results independent of the availability of previous results, I proposed the use of a simple machine-learning method (knn in this case) to roughly estimate an attainable performance. Such an estimation allows to relativize the real performance of a system for a given problem. Finally, I introduced the concept of local generality as a measure that can assess, or even reinforce, the global generalization capabilities of the fuzzy systems designed using Fuzzy CoCo.

6 Extensions of the Methodology

As mentioned in Section 5.1, Fuzzy CoCo requires the user to define a maximum number of rules for a given run. However, for each problem there exists a range of ideal rule-base sizes, that is hard to determine. The user is thus obliged to find this range by trial and error. I propose in this chapter two extensions to Fuzzy CoCo, intended to simplify the task of finding an adequate size of the rule base.

The first extension, called Island Fuzzy CoCo, is based on the Island model [110, 115]. It takes advantage of the exploration performed separately by concurrent instances of Fuzzy CoCo, where each instance is set to search for systems of different sizes. Island Fuzzy CoCo is presented in Section 6.1. Section 6.2 presents the second extension, inspired by the iterative rule learning approach [30], and called Incremental Fuzzy CoCo. In this method, the number of rules of the sought-after system increases each time that evolution satisfies certain criteria. In this way, the search for more complex systems starts on the basis of some "good" individuals.

6.1 Island Fuzzy CoCo

Often, when solving a fuzzy modeling problem, several instances of Fuzzy CoCo (in many cases running simultaneously on separated machines) are set to search for systems with different numbers of rules. Observing many of these runs, I remarked two interesting trends showing that some individuals from a given run should be of interest for the population of other runs of different complexity (either simpler or more complex).:

- In simple runs (i.e., searching for small systems), occasionally systems appear with performance similar to those of more complex runs, but with the advantage of being smaller and sometimes with shorter rules.
- In complex runs (i.e., searching for large systems), systems often appear that effectively utilize less rules than the maximum allowed. Such systems exhibit fitness values similar or superior to those of the simpler runs corresponding to their effective number of rules.

Island Fuzzy CoCo, the approach proposed herein, is similar to the so-called *island model* where several (sub)populations, called *islands* or *demes*, evolving separately most of the time, occasionally exchange individuals according to a certain

C.A. Peña Reyes: Coevolutionary Fuzzy Modeling, LNCS 3204, pp. 103-115, 2004.
© Springer-Verlag Berlin Heidelberg 2004

migration policy [110, 115]. Below, I sketch Island Fuzzy CoCo and describe two preliminary tests performed to explore its behavior.

6.1.1 The Proposed Algorithm

Several instances of Fuzzy CoCo—called islands—with different levels of complexity run concurrently. Contrary to the classic island model, in which the genomes of the individuals of all the islands are compatible, in Island Fuzzy CoCo individuals from different islands cannot reproduce directly as their genomes encode a different number of rules. A controlled migratory flux, adapted to the model, allows individuals to pass from an island to another as illustrated in Figure 6.1.

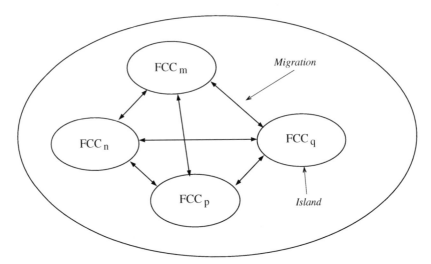

Fig. 6.1. Island Fuzzy CoCo. Several instances of Fuzzy CoCo, called here FCC_c, run concurrently. The index c represents the number of rules of the systems evolving in the island. The exchange of individuals (migration) is controlled by a migration policy, which in this example allows exchange of individuals between all the islands.

Migration introduces three new groups of parameters to be defined: the *migration topology*, i.e., a set of allowed migration paths; the *migration interval* (G_m), i.e., the number of generations between exchanges; and the *migration size* (N_m), i.e., the number of individuals that migrate between the islands. In other words, from time to time, each island proposes interesting candidates to some other islands and chooses a number of immigrants among the candidates proposed to it. Figure 6.2 presents the Island Fuzzy CoCo algorithm in pseudo-code format.

The main criterion to select the N_m migrants for a given destination island is the relative performance with respect to the actual performance of the population in the destination island. Two possible criteria, for an island, to select its N_m immigrants from a pool of candidates (M_D) are: (1) relative performance with respect to

begin Island Fuzzy CoCo
    g=0
    for each island I
        Initialize Fuzzy CoCo population $P_I(0)$
    end for
    while not done **do**
        for each island I
            Evaluate population
            g=g+1
            if migration interval G_m elapsed
                for each destination island D
                    M_D^I = Select-emigrants$[P_D(\text{g-1})]$
                    M_D^I = Adapt-genome$[M_D^I]$
                    send M_D^I to D
                end for
                $P_I'(g-1)$ = Reduce$[P_I(g-1)]$
                $P_I'(g)$ = Fuzzy-CoCo evolve $P_I'(g-1)$
                M_I' = Select-immigrants$[M_I]$
                $P_I(g)$ = $P_I'(g) + M_I'(g)$
            else
                $P_I(g)$ = Fuzzy-CoCo evolve $P_I(g-1)$
            end if
            Evaluate population $P_I(g)$
        end for
    end while
end Island Fuzzy CoCo

Fig. 6.2. Pseudo-code of Island Fuzzy CoCo. In each island an instance of Fuzzy CoCo runs for a given number of rules. Every G_m generations, each island propose N_m emigrants to other islands (called here M_D^I) and chooses N_m immigrants from the pool of candidates proposed to it ($M_I = \sum_j (M_I^j)$). "Fuzzy-CoCo evolve" corresponds to the evolutionary operators applied in Fuzzy CoCo.

the actual average performance in the island and (2) keep a balanced immigration either by choosing the same number of immigrants from each origin island, or by establishing a maximum number of migrants per origin island. Even though each island may use its own, specific fitness criteria to evaluate its individuals, migrants must be selected on the basis of a common fitness measure (e.g., performance).

Given that the complexity of individuals in the origin and the destination islands are different, the genome of the migrants must be adapted: eliminating unused rules in downsizing migrants or duplicating active rules for enlarging migrants. Special care must be taken to preserve as much as possible the fitness of the migrants after these operations.

Fuzzy CoCo involves two coevolving species, but migration is decided according to the fitness computed for entire fuzzy systems consisting of a pair (*individual-cooperator*). Besides, the complexity of the system, which is a key concept in Island Fuzzy CoCo, is based only on individuals from the rules species. There exist thus at least three possible ways to choose the migrants: (1) migrants are chosen separately for each species according to their fitness independent of their relation with the other species; (2) migrants are chosen for each species, but emigrate together with their cooperators (i.e., selected members of the other species), and (3) migrants are selected only from the rule species and migrate together with their cooperators.

6.1.2 Preliminary Tests of Island Fuzzy CoCo

I present herein some tests of Island Fuzzy CoCo on the Iris-classifier and the WBCD problems, for which adequate setups of Fuzzy CoCo are already known. The main goal of these tests is to explore the role of two of the new migration parameters: interval and size. I first used the Iris classifier problem (Section 3.4) obtaining good results, but the low number of rules required for this problem and the consequent low volume of data, render difficult the extraction of conclusions. I thus used the WBCD problem (Section 4.1) that offers a wider range of complexity. (Note: Part of the Iris-classifier tests were performed in the frame of a student project by Yves Blatter.)

6.1.2.1 Experimental Setup. Setting up Island Fuzzy CoCo requires the definition of the following parameters:

- Number of islands and number of rules of their individuals. Based on the previous experience, I set 4 islands for the Iris classifier problem, whose individuals encode systems going from two to five rules. For the WBCD problem, individuals distributed in seven islands encoded systems going from one rule to seven rules.
- Fuzzy CoCo setup. All the islands use the same setup. Table 6.1 delineates the values used for the Fuzzy CoCo parameters in each problem.

Table 6.1. Fuzzy CoCo set-up used for the Iris classifier and the WBCD problems.

Parameter	Iris	WBCD
Population size $\|Ps\|$	70	50
Maximum generations G_{max}	1000	1500
Crossover probability P_c	1	1
Mutation probability P_m	0.1	0.1
Elitism rate E_r	0.2	0.2
"Fit" cooperators N_{cf}	1	1
Random cooperators N_{cr}	1	1

- Migration topology. All the possible migratory paths are allowed.
- Migration interval G_m and migration size N_m. These are the parameters under study. To test the migration effect I used three values for each parameter (for a total of 9 possible combinations). The values for the Iris classifier problem are $G_m = \{1, 10, 100\}$ generations and $N_m = \{5, 20, 50\}$ individuals. For the WBCD problems the values are $G_m = \{1, 5, 50\}$ generations and $N_m = \{2, 5, 20\}$ individuals.

- Emigrant selection. The pool of possible emigrants to a given island is composed of individuals whose fitness value is greater than the actual average fitness of the destination island. For each destination island, up to N_m emigrants are selected fitness-proportionally from each species. Note that migrants carry with them their cooperators. However, if several individuals carry the same cooperator, only one copy of the cooperator is placed in the migrating group.
- Immigrant selection. The pool of possible immigrants to an island consists of all the candidates proposed to it that exhibit a fitness value greater than the actual average fitness on the island. Each island selects up to N_m immigrants using fitness-proportionate selection. No mechanism to balance immigration is applied.
- Fitness function. All the islands use the same fitness function for both evolution and migration purposes. The Iris classifier islands simply use the classification performance F_c. The fitness function of the WBCD islands includes an interpretability-related term. It is given by $F = F_c - \alpha F_v$, where $\alpha = 0.0015$, F_c is the classification performance, and F_v penalizes systems with a large number of variables in their rules.

6.1.2.2 Results for the Iris Classifier Problem. Ten different tests were performed: nine combinations of migration parameters and a control test without migration. Ten runs were performed for each case, for a total of 100 runs (each with four islands). Table 6.2 presents the average fitness for each test. All the tests succeed in finding systems exhibiting the maximum fitness (i.e., $F_c = 99.33\%$).

Table 6.2. Results of Island Fuzzy CoCo for the Iris classifier problem. Shown below are the average, over ten runs, of the maximum fitness obtained for each combination of the migration parameters: migration interval G_m and migration size N_m expressed in generations and individuals, respectively.

G_m	N_m		
	5	20	50
1	98.59%	98.53%	98.60%
10	98.73%	98.67%	98.80%
100	98.73%	**98.93%**	98.73%
None		98.83%	

From the analysis of these global results—i.e., extracting the best system found at each run—one can not see that migration affords a real advantage with respect to simple Fuzzy CoCo (i.e., without migration). Only those runs that allow 20 migrants every 100 generations perform slightly better. However, as Island Fuzzy CoCo searches simultaneously for different system sizes, it is necessary to analyze the results for each island. Figure 6.3 compares, island by island, the results obtained using the best migration policy with those obtained without migration.

Migration appears to have a benefical effect for those islands containing large systems. However, the low number of islands required for this problem renders difficult the extraction of conclusions.

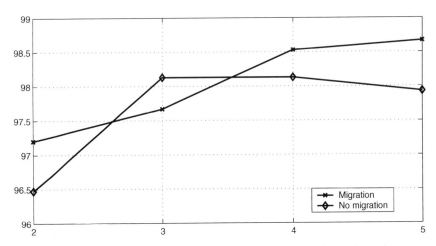

Fig. 6.3. Results, island by island, for the Iris classifier problem. The figure shows the average fitness obtained, for each number of rules, using the best migration policy (i.e., $G_m = 100$ generations and $N_m = 20$ individuals), compared with those obtained without migration.

6.1.2.3 Results for the WBCD Problem. Ten different tests were performed—i.e., nine combinations of migration parameters and a control test without migration. Five runs were performed for each case, for a total of 50 runs (each with seven islands). Tables 6.3.a and b present, respectively, the average and the best fitness for each test.

Table 6.3. Results of Island Fuzzy CoCo for the WBCD problem. Shown below are (a) the average over ten runs and (b) the maximum fitness, obtained for each combination of the tested migration parameters: migration interval G_m and migration size N_m expressed in generations and individuals, respectively.

(a) Average fitness				(b) Best fitness			
G_m		N_m		G_m		N_m	
	2	5	20		2	5	20
1	97.93%	97.73%	97.98%	1	**98.14%**	97.82%	**98.14%**
5	97.90%	97.94%	97.98%	5	97.99%	97.99%	**98.14%**
50	**98.00%**	**98.01%**	**98.06%**	50	98.12%	98.12%	**98.41%**
None		97.98%		None		98.12%	

From these global results, one can see that only those runs using either $G_m = 50$ or $N_m = 20$ find systems with similar performance to those found without migration. Runs combining both values find the best systems. To evaluate the effect that migration has on each island, Figure 6.4 compares the results of the best migration policy with those obtained without migration.

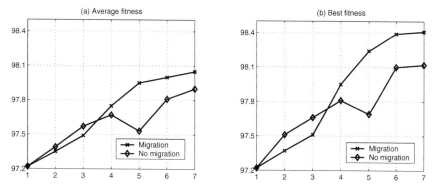

Fig. 6.4. Results, island by island, for the WBCD problem. The figure shows the average fitness obtained, for each number of rules, using the best migration policy (i.e., $G_m = 50$ generations and $N_m = 20$ individuals), compared with those obtained without migration.

These results confirm, as observed in the Iris-classifier test, that an adequate migration policy may have a clearly positive effect on the performance of islands containing complex individuals. In this case four-rule to seven-rule systems.

Migration also affects the dynamics of evolution in each island. Figure 6.5 shows the evolution of performance in different islands with and without migration. Note that even for small systems, where migration does not improve the final performance, the fitness evolve at least as fast as in the absence of migration.

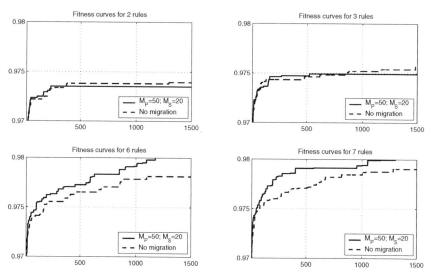

Fig. 6.5. Effect of migration on evolutionary dynamics. The figure shows the average fitness in different islands with and without migration. The abscissa represents the number of generations.

6.1.2.4 Analysis of Results. The tests presented above constitute a first exploration of the method. One can, however, advance some conclusions that should be verified with further tests.

- Migration has positive effects, with respect to simple Fuzzy CoCo, on the global search capabilities and on the evolutionary dynamics; in particular, for islands containing systems with a high number of rules.
- Island Fuzzy CoCo exhibits slightly lower search power for smaller systems. This may be due to the use of identical setups for all the islands, tailored to high-complexity islands.
- The setup of Island Fuzzy CoCo may be difficult. First, because of the new migratory parameters that enlarge the number of parameters to be defined by the user. And second, because each island should require specific setups, both migratory and coevolutionary, to perform optimally. However, the heuristics, presented in Section 5.2.6, to set Fuzzy CoCo up may alleviate this task.
- Due to migration requirements, Island Fuzzy CoCo is slightly heavier in computational resources than the corresponding multiple search with Fuzzy CoCo. However, as the results are obtained in less generations, for equivalent computational efforts, Island Fuzzy CoCo performs better than Fuzzy CoCo.
- Island Fuzzy CoCo should be implemented in parallel platforms, with each island executed on a separate processor. The communication between the islands is sparse as it is reduced to information about some migrants (i.e., genome and fitness value) and about the global performance of island populations.
- The principle of Island Fuzzy CoCo, i.e., the use of islands containing individuals with different levels of complexity, may be used for other optimization methods dealing with variable complexity (e.g., the evolution of finite state machines [59] and the evolution of fuzzy systems with different input-space dimensions [93]).

6.2 Incremental Fuzzy CoCo

Island Fuzzy CoCo—presented in Section 6.1—tackles the problem of finding an adequate size of the rule base by performing concurrent evolutionary searches with different sizes. It is better than Fuzzy CoCo for designing large systems, probably due to the information gathered in low-complexity islands and shared through migration. It is, however, costly in computational resources.

I propose thus an alternative, computationally cheaper, method inspired by the iterative rule learning approach (see Section 2.2.2) [30], in which a single instance of Fuzzy CoCo is used to search for fuzzy systems whose complexity increases as evolution advances. In contrast to iterative rule learning methods, individuals in Incremental Fuzzy CoCo represent entire fuzzy systems instead of one-rule systems. Below, I delineate Incremental Fuzzy CoCo and describe a first test performed to explore its potential search capabilities..

6.2.1 The Proposed Algorithm

Incremental Fuzzy CoCo starts as a simple instance of Fuzzy CoCo, used to search for small fuzzy systems (i.e., with a reduced number of rules, usually one). This instance runs until evolution satisfies a given criterion. At this point, part of the evolved population is used to seed the initial population of a new instance of Fuzzy CoCo. This new instance, that is set up to search for larger systems, runs until a new criterion is satisfied and a new instance with larger individuals is launched. The process is repeated until a termination criterion is satisfied. Due to the change of complexity, the genomes must be adapted before their use in a new instance of Fuzzy CoCo. Figure 6.6 presents the Island Fuzzy CoCo algorithm in pseudo-code format.

begin Incremental Fuzzy CoCo
    $R = R_{min}$
    Initialize Fuzzy CoCo populations for R rules $P_R(0)$
    while not done **do**
        while increment criterion not satisfied **do**
            Run Fuzzy CoCo: $P_R = FCC(P_R(0))$
            $P_R(0) = P_R$
        end while
        $Q_R = \text{Select-seed}[P_R]$
        $R' = R + R_{inc}$
        $Q'_R = \text{Adapt-genome}[Q_R]$
        $P'_R(0) = \text{complete } Q'_R \text{ with random individuals with } R' \text{ rules}$
        $R = R'$
    end while
end Incremental Fuzzy CoCo

Fig. 6.6. Pseudo-code of Incremental Fuzzy CoCo. A simple Fuzzy CoCo evolves a population of systems of size R. Each time an increment criterion is satisfied, the sought-after complexity is increased and part of the population is used to seed a new instance of Fuzzy CoCo.

The criteria used to decide to increase the complexity may be one or more of the following: number of generations elapsed, average performance of the entire population or of a selected elite, stagnation of evolution, or explicit user interaction. A part of the actual population is used to seed the new, complexity-increased, population. Due to the increased complexity in the new population, the genome of the selected seed must be adapted by duplicating some active rules. Special care must be taken to ensure that fitness is preserved after this operation. The remaining individuals in the initial population are generated randomly. In this way it is possible to keep the flexibility of the search while launching the new search with known "good individuals."

6.2.2 Testing Incremental Fuzzy CoCo

I present herein a first test of Incremental Fuzzy CoCo performed on the WBCD database. The main goal of this test is to verify the potential search capabilities of the method.

6.2.2.1 Experimental Setup. Setting up Incremental Fuzzy CoCo requires the definition of the following parameters:

- Range of the number of rules. The algorithm starts with one-rule systems and works its way up to ten-rule systems.
- Increment criterion. Complexity is increased after a given number of generations. The number of generations allowed for each instance depends on the number of rules: it starts at 200 generations for one-rule systems and goes up to 400 generations for ten-rule systems.
- Fuzzy CoCo setup. All the instances of Fuzzy CoCo use the same setup. Table 6.4 delineates the values used for the Fuzzy CoCo parameters.

Table 6.4. Fuzzy CoCo set-up for all the instances in Incremental Fuzzy CoCo for the WBCD problem.

Parameter	Value
Population size $\|Ps\|$	100
Maximum generations G_{max}	1000
Crossover probability P_c	1
Mutation probability P_m	0.15
Elitism rate E_r	0.1
"Fit" cooperators N_{cf}	1
Random cooperators N_{cr}	1

- Number of seeding individuals. The best five percent of the evolved population—the elite—is used to seed the new initial population. For the rule species, the genomes are adapted to the new size by adding a new rule. Each individual of the selected elite is used to generate three new individuals: the first is obtained by duplicating one of the active rules, the other two by adding a random rule. The remaining individuals (i.e., 85% of the population) are randomly initialized. In this way, the first 5% are known to perform well, the following 10% explore promising regions of the new enlarged search space, while the remaining 85% explore new regions.

6.2.2.2 Results. Thirty-two runs were performed, all but one of which found systems whose classification performance exceeds 98.0%. In particular, considering the best individual per run (i.e., the evolved system with the highest classification success rate), 20 runs led to a fuzzy system whose performance exceeds 98.5%, and of these, 2 runs found systems whose performance exceeds 98.7%.; these results are summarized in Figure 6.7. The best system found obtains an overall classification rate of 98.83%. The average performance over the 32 runs is 98.50%. (Note:

The results presented here were obtained by Olivier Rutti in the course of a student project.)

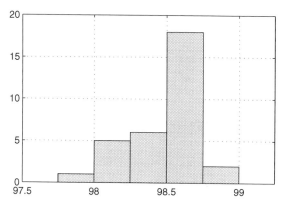

Fig. 6.7. Summary of results of 32 evolutionary runs. The histogram depicts the number of systems exhibiting a given classification performance level at the end of the evolutionary run.

Figure 6.8 shows the evolution of the classification performance during Incremental Fuzzy CoCo runs.

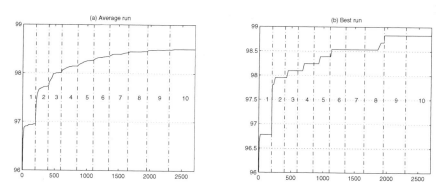

Fig. 6.8. Evolution of classification performance in Incremental Fuzzy CoCo. The figures show the classification performance for: (a) the average over 32 runs, and (b)the best run. The abscissa represents the number of generations elapsed. The numbers 1 to 10 represent the number of rules of the systems evolved in the corresponding interval.

Taking the results obtained by Incremental Fuzzy CoCo at the end of the search for seven-rule systems (corresponding to 1650 generations), we can compare them with the results of Fuzzy CoCo when searching for seven-rule systems presented in Section 4.1.2. Table 6.5 presents this comparison, while Figure 6.9 extends the comparison to other rule base sizes. The best systems found by Incremental Fuzzy CoCo are worse than those found by Fuzzy CoCo. However, the average performance of the former is better, and its results are obtained with less generations than those of the latter.

Table 6.5. Comparison of seven-rule systems evolved by Incremental Fuzzy CoCo with those obtained using Fuzzy CoCo.

	Generations	Average	Best
Incremental Fuzzy CoCo	1650	98.43%	98.54%
Simple Fuzzy CoCo	1700	98.25%	98.98%

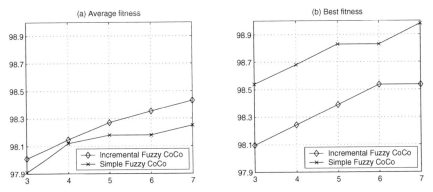

Fig. 6.9. Comparison of systems evolved by Incremental Fuzzy CoCo with those obtained using Fuzzy CoCo. The figure shows the classification performance obtained at the end of the search for each rule-base size.

6.2.2.3 Analysis of Results. The test presented above constitutes a very first approach to the method. The results suggest, however, some interesting features that deserve further exploration.

– Incremental Fuzzy CoCo seems to exhibit better repeatability than Fuzzy CoCo, as suggested by the narrow distribution of the results (see Figure 6.7). This is true not only for the global results but also for different rule-base sizes as shown in Figure 6.9. However, this approach fails to find top systems as good as those found by Fuzzy CoCo. One of the possible reasons is, again, that all the instances of Fuzzy CoCo were identically set up.
– The use of a fixed number of generations to define the increment of the complexity should be a weak criterion as the population can either converge toward mediocre performances, if this number is too high, or be stopped before a good exploration of the search space is performed, if this number is too low. This criterion affects directly the diversity and the quality of the initial population of the following instance.

– Intuitively, the seeding strategy (5% elite, 10% modified elite) is adequate, but the rate of seeding individuals needs to be tuned, as it should be excessive if the elite is not diverse enough.
– This method requires a deeper study to better understand the effects of the parameters (i.e., Fuzzy CoCo, increment criterion, and seeding strategy) on its performance. The goal of the study should be to find a setup that improves the quality of the best systems while preserving as much as possible the repeatability of the results.
– Even if this goal is not attained, Incremental Fuzzy CoCo can be useful, as it is, for:
    – searching automatically for an adequate range of sizes of the rule base, and
    – estimating attainable performance values for a given problem, and for different number of rules.

7 Conclusions and Future Work

7.1 Summary

I presented a novel approach for system design—Fuzzy CoCo—based on fuzzy logic and coevolutionary computation, which is conducive to explaining human decisions. My algorithm has been able to find accurate and interpretable systems for hard, real-world problems. The analysis of Fuzzy CoCo and of the systems it produced shows, among other features, the consistency of the results. I also proposed two extensions to the method, which deserve further exploration.

Evolutionary fuzzy modeling—i.e., the design of fuzzy inference systems using evolutionary algorithms—constitutes the methodological base of my work. In Chapter 2 I studied extant evolutionary fuzzy modeling approaches and some criteria and considerations involved in this task. I emphasized an aspect usually neglected in most approaches: interpretability. In particular, I presented some strategies to satisfy semantic and syntactic criteria that reinforce the interpretability of the systems produced. To illustrate these concepts, I applied a basic fuzzy-genetic approach to solve a medical diagnostic problem: the WBCD problem. The systems obtained were the best explanatory systems presented at the time for this problem.

The aforementioned study brought to the fore some limitations of evolutionary fuzzy modeling, but, at the same time, it provided clues on how to overcome them. Based on these clues, I proposed the use of cooperative coevolution to surmount the problem of dealing with different types of parameters in the same genome. This is the origin of Fuzzy CoCo, presented in detail in Chapter 3, together with a simple application example: the Iris classification problem. The systems obtained for this problem surpassed previous fuzzy modeling results.

Fuzzy CoCo was then used in Chapter 4 to model the decision processes involved in two breast-cancer diagnostic problems: the WBCD problem and the Catalonia mammography interpretation problem. For the WBCD problem, Fuzzy CoCo produced markedly better results using less or similar computational resources than the fuzzy-genetic approach. For the Catalonia problem, an evolved system was embedded within a web-based tool—called COBRA—for aiding radiologists in mammography interpretation.

In order to attain a deeper understanding of Fuzzy CoCo, I performed in Chapter 5 several analyses regarding the performance of the methodology and of the systems it produces. These analyses involve aspects like the application of the method,

C.A. Peña Reyes: Coevolutionary Fuzzy Modeling, LNCS 3204, pp. 117-121, 2004.
© Springer-Verlag Berlin Heidelberg 2004

the effects that some parameters have on performance, the consistency and the quality of the systems designed using Fuzzy CoCo, as well as their local generality. Finally, I proposed two extensions: Island Fuzzy CoCo and Incremental Fuzzy CoCo, which together with the original CoCo constitute a family of coevolutionary fuzzy modeling techniques. The extensions are intended to guide the choice of an adequate number of rules for a given problem—a critical, hard-to-define parameter of Fuzzy CoCo. The encouraging preliminary results obtained with these extensions motivate further investigation.

7.2 Original Contributions

To the best of my knowledge, this is the first work to analyze and develop in-depth the concept of coevolutionary fuzzy modeling. While this in itself constitutes an original achievement, it is not the only contribution of the present research to the state of the art. In this section, I will outline the most interesting original contributions.

– In Section 2.1, which studies the fuzzy modeling problem, I proposed a *novel classification of the parameters of fuzzy systems* into four classes: logic, structural, connective, and operational. This classification was used to decompose the fuzzy modeling problem and to analyze how existing modeling techniques dealt with it. These analyses provided some key ideas, important to the conception of Fuzzy CoCo. In particular, they served to show that most of the time the fuzzy modeling problem reduces to the design of connective and operational parameters, which are very different in nature. This fact led to the idea of applying cooperative coevolution.
– The interpretability considerations presented in Section 2.3 contain several original elements. First, observing that most of the interpretability criteria presented in the literature were mainly oriented toward constraining the definition of membership functions, I grouped them under the label *semantic criteria*, as they affect the coherence of the linguistic concepts. Then, I identified and proposed some other criteria regarding the rule base, which are called *syntactic criteria*, as they affect the (causal) connection between linguistic concepts. Finally, I proposed a set of *modeling strategies* that, when applied, should reinforce the linguistic integrity—both semantic and syntactic—of the fuzzy systems produced. Note that these considerations are valid for any fuzzy modeling technique.
– Chapter 3 introduced Fuzzy CoCo, a novel cooperative coevolutionary approach to fuzzy modeling. The idea of applying *cooperative coevolution* arose from the observation that the fuzzy modeling problem should be decomposed into (at least) two separated but related search processes: one for connective, the other for operational parameters. Cooperative coevolution succeeds in overcoming some limitations exhibited by standard evolutionary fuzzy modeling: stagnation, convergence to local optima, and computational costliness. Besides performance improvement, Fuzzy CoCo was designed with interpretability being a prime goal.

This was evidenced in the different applications of Fuzzy CoCo, where I applied the proposed interpretability strategies.

– The systems obtained to solve the Catalonia mammography problem (Section 4.2), served as a base for the *development of the COBRA system*—the Catalonia Online Breast-cancer Risk Assessor—a web-based tool for aiding radiologists in mammography interpretation.

– Finally, I proposed two extensions to Fuzzy CoCo, intended to simplify the task of finding an adequate size of the rule base. Two key elements of the first extension, *Island Fuzzy CoCo*, are: (1) the existence of evolutionary islands containing individuals of different sizes, and (2) a migration mechanism that adapts the size of the migrants to render them compatible with their destination island. The second extension, *Incremental Fuzzy CoCo*, bases its search power on a mechanism of incremental evolution. In contrast with iterative rule learning methods, the search does not set a good system early on. Good systems are only used to signal promising search regions as they seed the new initial population. These methods represent two new members of a family of coevolutionary fuzzy modeling techniques based on Fuzzy CoCo.

7.3 Future Work

Throughout this book I have suggested a number of possible directions for future research within the domain of coevolutionary fuzzy modeling, and particularly for the development of tools based on Fuzzy CoCo. In this section, I will briefly expand on some ideas.

Deepening and Improving the Methodology

In all the applications of Fuzzy CoCo described herein, the evolutionary algorithms for both species, membership functions and rules, were set up identically. However, a number of questions concerning this choice could be addressed in the future:

– Studying the effects of the evolutionary parameters on the performance of each species to determine specific optimal setups.

– Investigating other types of evolutionary algorithms for each species, for example, real-coded ones—such as evolution strategies—for membership-function species, or tree-based representations for rules species.

Exploration of Island Fuzzy CoCo

The encouraging performance of this algorithm in the preliminary tests (Section 6.1) invites further exploration. Future work on this algorithm should concentrate, among others, on the following issues:

- Tuning the setup, as the existence of migration between islands may change the effect of evolutionary parameters on performance. This means revisiting the analysis presented in Section 5.2.
- Defining a mechanism for dynamically finding the range of number of rules to perform the search, e.g., stopping islands that stagnate in low performance values or creating islands for larger individuals if performance suggests this being viable.
- Comparing the performance of Island Fuzzy CoCo with that of simple Fuzzy CoCo (i.e., with zero migration) on harder problems. The island version shows higher performance improvement for islands containing systems with a high number of rules. Given that harder problems usually require larger systems, the algorithm seems adequate to solve them.
- Parallel implementation. As mentioned before, the algorithm is well suited for parallelization, implementing each island on a separate processor. There is no need for central control, and the communication between the islands is reduced to information about some migrants (their genome and fitness values) and about the global performance of island populations.

Further Development of Incremental Fuzzy CoCo

Although this algorithm was explored only preliminarily, it obtained some promising results (Section 6.2). Future work on this algorithm could include:

- The setup of each instance of Fuzzy CoCo should be adapted to the features of the systems it evolves. Parameters such as population size, mutation probability, elitism rate, and number of cooperators should change as the complexity of the encoded systems increases.
- This method requires a more thorough study to better understand the effects on performance of its specific new parameters (i.e. increment criteria and seeding strategy).
- In the same way the complexity of the search is increased, there should exist some criteria to decrease this complexity. For example, if the effective number of rules used by (most of) the best systems is lower than the currently allowed maximum number of rules.

Development of a Fuzzy Modeling Toolbox

Several of the contributions afforded by this work could constitute elements for developing a fuzzy modeling toolbox based on the Fuzzy CoCo family.

- Incremental Fuzzy CoCo can serve for early exploration of the problem space. It can estimate both attainable performance values and an adequate range of sizes of the rule base.
- Island Fuzzy CoCo could explore in-depth the range of complexities found in order to validate the estimation obtained before.
- Simple Fuzzy CoCo could perform specific searches for systems with a given, user-defined number of rules.

– An extended version of the user interface developed for the COBRA system could serve for the interaction with both the fuzzy modeler and the end user.

Integration Within Knowledge-Engineering Environments

As mentioned in Chapter 1, knowledge engineering is the best alternative to designing large and hierarchic explanatory systems. However, this process usually involves many smaller modules whose design could well take advantage of the main modeling features of Fuzzy CoCo: high-performance, data-based, and interpretability-oriented.

Bibliography

1. J. T. Alander. An indexed bibliography of genetic algorithms with fuzzy logic. In Pedrycz [81], pages 299–318.
2. T. Bäck, U. Hammel, and H.-P. Schwefel. Evolutionary computation: Comments on the history and current state. *IEEE Transactions on Evolutionary Computation*, 1(1):3–17, April 1997.
3. Wolfgang Banzhaf, Peter Nordin, Robert E. Keller, and Frank D. Francone. *Genetic Programming – An Introduction; On the Automatic Evolution of Computer Programs and its Applications*. Morgan Kaufmann, dpunkt.verlag, January 1998.
4. K. P. Bennett and O. L. Mangasarian. Neural network training via linear programming. In P. M. Pardalos, editor, *Advances in Optimization and Parallel Computing*, pages 56–57. Elsevier Science, 1992.
5. C. L. Blake and C. J. Merz. UCI repository of machine learning databases, 1998.
6. C. Bonivento, A. Davalli, and C. Fantuzzi. Tuning of myoelectric prostheses using fuzzy logic. *Artificial Intelligence in Medicine*, 21(1–3):221–225, January–March 2001.
7. G. E. P. Box. Evolutionary operation: A method for increasing industrial productivity. *Applied Statistics*, 6(2):81–101, 1957.
8. G. E. P. Box and J. S. Hunter. Condensed calculations for evolutionary operation programs. *Technometrics*, 1:77–95, 1959.
9. H. Brenner. Measures of differential diagnostic value of diagnostic procedures. *Journal of Clinical Epidemiology*, 49(12):1435–1439, December 1996.
10. D. Chakraborty and N.R. Pal. Integrated feature analysis and fuzzy rule-based system identification in a neuro-fuzzy paradigm. *IEEE Transactions on Systems, Man, and Cybernetics, Part B: Cybernetics*, 31(3):391–400, June 2001.
11. B.-S. Chen, S.-C. Feng, and K.-C. Wang. Traffic modeling, prediction, and congestion control for high-speed networks: A fuzzy AR approach. *IEEE Transactions on Fuzzy Systems*, 8(5):491–508, October 2000.
12. O. Cordón, F. Herrera, and M. Lozano. On the combination of fuzzy logic and evolutionary computation: A short review and bibliography. In Pedrycz [81], pages 33–56.
13. P. Darwen and X. Yao. Every niching method has its niche: Fitness sharing and implicit sharing compared. In H.-M. Voigt, W. Ebeling, I. Rechenberg, and H.-P. Schwefel, editors, *Parallel Problem Solving from Nature – PPSN IV*, pages 398–407, Berlin, 1996. Springer.
14. W. Duch, R. Adamczak, and K. Grabczewski. A new methodology of extraction, optimization and application of crisp and fuzzy logical rules. *IEEE Transactions on Neural Networks*, 12(2):277–306, March 2001.
15. M. O. Efe and O. Kaynak. On stabilization of gradient-based training strategies for computationally intelligent systems. *IEEE-Transactions on Fuzzy Systems*, 8(5):564–575, October 2000.

16. M. O. Efe and O. Kaynak. A novel optimization procedure for training of fuzzy inference systems by combining variable structure systems technique and levenbergmarquardt algorithm. *Fuzzy Sets and Systems*, 122(1):153–165, August 2001.

17. R. Eriksson. Applying cooperative coevolution to inventory control parameter optimization. Master's thesis, University of Skövde, 1996.

18. J. Espinosa and J. Vandewalle. Constructing fuzzy models with linguistic integrity from numerical data-AFRELI algorithm. *IEEE Transactions on Fuzzy Systems*, 8(5):591–600, October 2000.

19. F. Fernandez, G. Galeano, and J. A. Gomez. Comparing synchronous and asynchronous parallel and distributed GP models. In E. Lutton, J. A. Foster, J. Miller, C. Ryan, and A. G. B. Tettamanzi, editors, *Proceedings of the 4th European Conference on Genetic Programming, EuroGP 2002*, volume 2278 of *LNCS*, pages 327–336, Kinsale, Ireland, 3-5 April 2002. Springer-Verlag.

20. R. A. Fisher. The use of multiple measurements in taxonomic problems. *Annals of Eugenics*, 7:179–188, 1936.

21. M. Si Fodil, P. Siarry, F. Guely, and J.-L. Tyran. A fuzzy rule base for the improved control of a pressurized water nuclear reactor. *IEEE Transactions on Fuzzy Systems*, 8(1):1–10, February 2000.

22. D. B. Fogel, editor. *Evolutionary Computation: The Fossil Record*. IEEE Press, Piscataway, NJ, 1998.

23. D. B. Fogel. *Evolutionary Computation: Toward a New Philosophy of Machine Intelligence*. IEEE Press, Piscataway, NJ, second edition, 1999.

24. L. J. Fogel. Autonomous automata. *Industrial Research*, 4:14–19, 1962.

25. L. J. Fogel, A. J. Owens, and M. J. Walsh. *Artificial Intelligence through Simulated Evolution*. John Wiley & Sons, New York, 1966.

26. R. M. Friedberg. A learning machine: I. *IBM Journal of Research and Development*, 2:2–13, 1958.

27. R. M. Friedberg, B. Dunham, and J. H. North. A learning machine. II. *IBM Journal of Research and Development*, 3:282–287, 1959.

28. D. E. Goldberg. *Genetic Algorithms in Search, Optimization, and Machine Learning*. Addison-Wesley, Reading, Mass., 1989.

29. S. Guillaume. Designing fuzzy inference systems from data: An interpretability-oriented review. *IEEE Transactions on Fuzzy Systems*, 9(3):426–443, June 2001.

30. F. Herrera, M. Lozano, and J. L. Verdegay. Generating fuzzy rules from examples using genetic algorithms. In B. Bouchon-Meunier, R. R. Yager, and L. A. Zadeh, editors, *Fuzzy Logic and Soft Computing*, pages 11–20. World Scientific, 1995.

31. W. Daniel Hillis. Co-evolving parasites improve simulated evolution as an optimization procedure. *Physica D*, 42:228–234, 1990. Proceedings of the Ninth Annual Int. Conf. of the Center for Nonlinear Studies, Ed. Stephanie Forrest.

32. J. H. Holland. Outline for a logical theory of adaptive systems. *Journal of the ACM*, 9(3):297–314, July 1962.

33. J. H. Holland. Processing and processors for schemata. In E. L. Jacks, editor, *Associative information processing*, pages 127–146. New York: American Elsevier, 1971.

34. J. H. Holland. *Adpatation in Natural and Artificial Systems*. University of Michigan Press, Ann Arbor, MI, 1975.

35. T. P. Hong and J. B. Chen. Processing individual fuzzy attributes for fuzzy rule induction. *Fuzzy Sets and Systems*, 112(1):127–140, May 2000.

36. Jörn Hopf. Cooperative coevolution of fuzzy rules. In N. Steele, editor, *Proceedings of the 2nd International ICSC Symposium on Fuzzy Logic and Applications (ISFL-97)*, pages 377–381, Zurich, Switzerland, 1997. ICSC Academic Press.

37. C. A. Hung and S. F. Lin. An incremental learning neural network for pattern classification. *International Journal of Pattern Recognition and Artificial Intelligence*, 13(6):913–928, September 1999.

38. P. Husbands and F. Mill. Simulated co-evolution as the mechanism for emergent planning and scheduling. In R. Belew and K. Booker, editors, *Proceedings of the 4th International Conference on Genetic Algorithms*, pages 264–270, San Diego, CA, July 1991. Morgan Kaufmann.

39. H. Ishibushi, T. Nakashima, and T. Murata. Performance evaluation of fuzzy classifier systems for multidimensional pattern classification problems. *IEEE Transactions on Systems, Man, and Cybernetics. Part B: Cybernetics*, 29(5):601–618, October 1999.

40. J.-S. R. Jang and C.-T. Sun. Neuro-fuzzy modeling and control. *Proceedings of the IEEE*, 83(3):378–406, March 1995.

41. Jonghyeok Jeong and Se-Young Oh. Automatic rule gerenartion for fuzzy logic controllers using rule-level coevolution of subpopulations. In *1999 Congress on Evolutionary Computation*, pages 2151–2156, Piscataway, NJ, 1999. IEEE Service Center.

42. Y. Jin. Fuzzy modeling of high-dimensional systems: complexity reduction and interpretability improvement. *IEEE Transactions on Fuzzy Systems*, 8(2):335–344, April 2000.

43. C.-F. Juang, J.-Y. Lin, and C.-T. Lin. Genetic reinforcement learning through symbiotic evolution for fuzzy controller design. *IEEE Transactions on Systems, Man and Cybernetics, Part B: Cybernetics*, 30(2):290–302, April 2000.

44. H. Juillé. *Methods for Statistical Inference: Extending the Evolutionary Computation Paradigm*. PhD thesis, Brandeis University, May 1999.

45. H.-B. Jun, C.-S. Joung, and K.-B. Sim. Co-evolution of fuzzy rules and membership functions. In *Proceedings of 3rd Asian Fuzzy Systems Symposium (AFSS'98)*, 1998.

46. C. L. Karr. Genetic algorithms for fuzzy controllers. *AI Expert*, 6(2):26–33, February 1991.

47. C. L. Karr, L. M. Freeman, and D. L. Meredith. Improved fuzzy process control of spacecraft terminal rendezvous using a genetic algorithm. In G. Rodriguez, editor, *Proceedings of Intelligent Control and Adaptive Systems Conference*, volume 1196, pages 274–288. SPIE, February 1990.

48. J. R. Koza. Genetic programming: A paradigm for genetically breeding populations of computer programs to solve problems. Technical Report STAN-CS-90-1314, Dept. of Computer Science, Stanford University, June 1990.

49. J. R. Koza. *Genetic Programming*. The MIT Press, Cambridge, MA, 1992.

50. C.-T. Lin and C. S. G. Lee. Neural-network-based fuzzy logic control and decision system. *IEEE Transactions on Computers*, 40(12):1320–1336, December 1991.

51. P. Lindskog. Fuzzy identification from a grey box modeling point of view. In H. Hellendoorn and D. Driankov, editors, *Fuzzy Model Identification*, pages 3–50. Springer-Verlag, 1997.

52. Y.L. Loukas. Adaptive neuro-fuzzy inference system: An instant and architecture-free predictor for improved QSAR studies. *Journal of Medicinal Chemistry*, 44(17):2772–2783, August 2001.

53. E. H. Mamdani. Application of fuzzy algorithms for control of a simple dynamic plant. *Proceedings of the IEE*, 121(12):1585–1588, 1974.

54. E. H. Mamdani and S. Assilian. An experiment in linguistic synthesis with a fuzzy logic controller. *International Journal of Man-Machine Studies*, 7(1):1–13, 1975.

55. O. L. Mangasarian, R. Setiono, and W.-H Goldberg. Pattern recognition via linear programming: Theory and application to medical diagnosis. In T. F. Coleman and Y. Li, editors, *Large-Scale Numerical Optimization*, pages 22–31. SIAM, 1990.

56. O. L. Mangasarian, W. N. Street, and W. H. Wolberg. Breast cancer diagnosis and prognosis via linear programming. Mathematical Programming Technical Report 94-10, University of Wisconsin, 1994.

57. J. M. Mendel. Fuzzy logic systems for engineering: A tutorial. *Proceedings of the IEEE*, 83(3):345–377, March 1995.

58. C. J. Merz and P. M. Murphy. UCI repository of machine learning databases, 1996.

59. B. Mesot, C. A. Peña-Reyes E. Sanchez, and A. Pérez-Uribe. SOS++: Finding smart behaviors using learning and evolution. In R. K. Standish, M. A. Bedau, and H. A. Abbass, editors, *Artificial Life VIII. The 8th International Conference on the Simulation and Synthesis of Living Systems*, pages 264–273. The MIT Press, 2002.

60. Z. Michalewicz. *Genetic Algorithms + Data Structures = Evolution Programs*. Springer-Verlag, Heidelberg, third edition, 1996.

61. M. Mitchell. *An Introduction to Genetic Algorithms*. MIT Press, Cambridge, MA, 1996.

62. S. Mitra and Y. Hayashi. Neuro-fuzzy rule generation: Survey in soft computing framework. *IEEE Transactions on Neural Networks*, 11(3):748–768, May 2000.

63. D. E. Moriarty. *Symbiotic Evolution of Neural Networks in Sequential Decision Tasks*. PhD thesis, University of Texas, Austin, 1997.

64. D. Nauck and R. Kruse. A neuro-fuzzy method to learn fuzzy classification rules from data. *Fuzzy Sets and Systems*, 89(3):277–288, August 1997.

65. D. Nauck and R. Kruse. Neuro-fuzzy systems for function approximation. *Fuzzy Sets and Systems*, 101(2):261–271, January 1999.

66. B. N. Nelson. Automatic vehicle detection in infrared imagery using a fuzzy inference-based classification system. *IEEE-Transaction on Fuzzy Systems*, 9:53–61, February 2001.

67. T. Niwa and M. Tanaka. Analysis on the island model parallel genetic algorithms for the genetic drifts. In B. McKay, X. Yao, C. S. Newton, J.-H. Kim, and T. Furuhashi, editors, *Proceedings of the 2nd Asia-Pacific Conference on Simulated Evolution and Learning (SEAL-98)*, volume 1585 of *LNAI*, pages 349–356, Berlin, November 24–27 1999. Springer.

68. S. Nolfi and D. Floreano. Co-evolving predator and prey robots: Do 'arm races' arise in artificial evolution? *Artificial Life*, 4(4):311–335, 1998.

69. P. Nordin. *Evolutionary Program Induction of Binary Machine Code and its Application*. Krehl Verlag, Munster, Germany, 1997.

70. C.W. Omlin, L. Giles, and K.K. Thornber. Fuzzy knowledge and recurrent neural networks: A dynamical systems perspective. *Hybrid Neural Systems. Lecture Notes in Artificial Intelligence*, 1778:123–143, 2000.

71. S. G. Orel, N. Kay, C. Reynolds, and D. C. Sullivan. Bi-rads categorization as a predictor of malignancy. *Radiology*, 211(3):845–880, June 1999.

72. J. Paredis. Coevolutionary computation. *Artificial Life*, 2:355–375, 1995.

73. C. A. Peña-Reyes and M. Sipper. Evolving fuzzy rules for breast cancer diagnosis. In *Proceedings of 1998 International Symposium on Nonlinear Theory and Applications (NOLTA'98)*, volume 2, pages 369–372. Presses Polytechniques et Universitaires Romandes, Lausanne, 1998.

74. C. A. Peña-Reyes and M. Sipper. Designing breast cancer diagnostic systems via a hybrid fuzzy-genetic methodology. In *1999 IEEE International Fuzzy Systems Conference Proceedings*, volume 1, pages 135–139. IEEE Neural Network Council, 1999.

75. C. A. Peña-Reyes and M. Sipper. A fuzzy-genetic approach to breast cancer diagnosis. *Artificial Intelligence in Medicine*, 17(2):131–155, October 1999.

76. C. A. Peña-Reyes and M. Sipper. The flowering of Fuzzy CoCo: Evolving fuzzy iris classifiers. In V. Kurková, N. C. Steele, R. Neruda, and M. Kárný, editors, *Proceedings of the 5th International Conference on Artificial Neural Networks and Genetic Algorithms (ICANNGA 2001)*, pages 304–307. Springer-Verlag, 2001.

77. C. A. Peña-Reyes and M. Sipper. Fuzzy CoCo: A cooperative-coevolutionary approach to fuzzy modeling. *IEEE Transactions on Fuzzy Systems*, 9(5):727–737, October 2001.

78. C.-A. Peña-Reyes and M. Sipper. Combining evolutionary and fuzzy techniques in medical diagnosis. In M. Schmitt, H. N. Teodorescu, A. Jain, A. Jain, S. Jain, and L. C. Jain, editors, *Computational Intelligence Techniques in Medical Diagnosis and Prognosis*, volume 96 of *Studies in Fuzziness and Soft Computing*, chapter 14, pages 391–426. Springer-Verlag, Heidelberg, 2002.

79. C.-A. Peña-Reyes and M. Sipper. Fuzzy CoCo: Balancing accuracy and interpretability of fuzzy models by means of coevolution. In J. Casillas, O. Cordón, F. Herrera, and L. Magdalena, editors, *Accuracy Improvements in Linguistic Fuzzy Modeling*, volume 129 of *Studies in Fuzziness and Soft Computing*, pages 119–146. Physica-Verlag, 2003.

80. C. A. Peña-Reyes, M. Sipper, and L. Prieto. Sensitive, specific, and interpretable: Evolving a fuzzy mammographic-interpretation assessment tool. In *2002 IEEE International Fuzzy Systems Conference Proceedings*, pages 837–842. IEEE Neural Network Society, 2002.

81. W. Pedrycz, editor. *Fuzzy Evolutionary Computation*. Kluwer Academic Publishers, 1997.

82. W. Pedrycz and J. Valente de Oliveira. Optimization of fuzzy models. *IEEE Transactions on Systems, Man and Cybernetics, Part B: Cybernetics*, 26(4):627–636, August 1996.

83. R. Poli. Introduction to evolutionary computation. http://www.cs.bham.ac.uk/˜rmp-/slide_book/, October 1996. visited: 16 March 1999.

84. L. Porta, R. Villa, E. Andia, and E. Valderrama. Infraclinic breast carcinoma: Application of neural networks techniques for the indication of radioguided biopsias. In J. Mira, R. Moreno-Díaz, and J. Cabestany, editors, *Biological and Artificial Computation: From Neuroscience to Technology*, volume 1240 of *Lecture Notes in Computer Science*, pages 978–985. Springer, 1997.

85. M. A. Potter. *The Design and Analysis of a Computational Model of Cooperative Coevolution*. PhD thesis, George Mason University, 1997.

86. M. A. Potter and K. A. De Jong. A cooperative coevolutionary approach to function optimization. In Yuval Davidor, Hans-Paul Schwefel, and Reinhard Männer, editors, *Parallel Problem Solving from Nature – PPSN III*, pages 249–257, Berlin, 1994. Springer. Lecture Notes in Computer Science 866.

87. M. A. Potter and K. A. De Jong. Evolving neural networks with collaborative species. In *Proc. of the 1995 Summer Computer Simulation Conf.*, pages 340–345. The Society of Computer Simulation, 1995.

88. M. A. Potter and K. A. De Jong. Cooperative coevolution: An architecture for evolving coadapted subcomponents. *Evolutionary Computation*, 8(1):1–29, spring 2000.

89. M. A. Potter, K. A. De Jong, and J. J. Grefenstette. A coevolutionary approach to learning sequential decision rules. In Larry J. Eshelman, editor, *Proceedings of the 6th International Conference on Genetic Algorithms (ICGA95)*, pages 366–372. Morgan Kaufmann Publishers, 1995.

90. W. K. Purves, G. H. Orians, H. C. Heller, and D. Sadava. *Life. The Science of Biology*, chapter 52: Community Ecology. Sinauer, 5th edition, 1998.

91. I. Rechenberg. Cybernetic solution path of an experimental problem. Farborough Hants: Royal Aircraft Establishment. Library Translation 1122, August 1965. English Translation of lecture given at the Annual Conference of the WGLR at Berlin in September, 1964.

92. I. Rechenberg. *Evolutionsstrategie: Optimierung technischer Systeme nach Prinzipien der biologischen Evolution*. Frommann-Holzboog, Stuttgart, 1973.

93. I. Rojas, J. Gonzalez, H. Pomares, F.J. Rojas, F.J. Fernández, and A. Prieto. Multi-dimensional and multideme genetic algorithms for the construction of fuzzy systems. *International Journal of Approximate Reasoning*, 26:179–210, 2001.

94. I. Rojas, H. Pomares, J. Ortega, and A. Prieto. Self-organized fuzzy system generation from training examples. *IEEE Transactions on Fuzzy Systems*, 8(1):23–36, February 2000.

95. C. D. Rosin and R. K. Belew. New methods for competitive coevolution. *Evolutionary Computation*, 5(1):1–29, 1997.

96. M. Russo. FuGeNeSys - A fuzzy genetic neural system for fuzzy modeling. *IEEE Transactions on Fuzzy Systems*, 6(3):373–388, August 1998.

97. A. Lo Schiavo and A. M. Luciano. Powerful and flexible fuzzy algorithm for nonlinear dynamic system identification. *IEEE-Transaction on Fuzzy Systems*, 9:828–835, December 2001.

98. H.-P. Schwefel. Kybernetische evolution als strategie der experimentelen forschung in der stromungstechnik. Master's thesis, Technical University of Berlin, Hermann Föttinger Institute for Hydrodynamics, March 1965.

99. H.-P. Schwefel. *Evolutionsstrategie und numerische Optimierung*. PhD thesis, Technical University of Berlin, Department of Process Engineering, Berlin, May 1975.

100. H.-P. Schwefel. *Evolution and Optimum Seeking*. Sixth-Generation Computer Technology Series. John Wiley & Sons., New York, 1995.

101. R. Setiono. Extracting rules from pruned neural networks for breast cancer diagnosis. *Artificial Intelligence in Medicine*, 8:37–51, 1996.

102. R. Setiono. Generating concise and accurate classification rules for breast cancer diagnosis. *Artificial Intelligence in Medicine*, 18(3):205 – 219, 2000.

103. R. Setiono and H. Liu. Symbolic representation of neural networks. *IEEE Computer*, 29(3):71–77, March 1996.

104. M. Setnes. Supervised fuzzy clustering for rule extraction. *IEEE Transactions on Fuzzy Systems*, 8(4):416–424, August 2000.

105. Y. Shi, R. Eberhart, and Y. Chen. Implementation of evolutionary fuzzy systems. *IEEE Transactions on Fuzzy Systems*, 7(2):109–119, April 1999.

106. M. Sugeno and G. T. Kang. Structure identification of fuzzy model. *Fuzzy Sets and Systems*, 28(1):15–33, 1988.

107. I. Taha and J. Ghosh. Evaluation and ordering of rules extracted from feedforward networks. In *Proceedings of the IEEE International Conference on Neural Networks*, pages 221–226, 1997.

108. Y. Takagi and M. Sugeno. Fuzzy Identification of Systems and Its Applications to Modeling and Control. *IEEE Transactions on Systems, Man and Cybernetics*, 15:116–132, 1985.

109. A. Tettamanzi and M. Tomassini. Evolutionary algorithms and their applications. In D. Mange and M. Tomassini, editors, *Bio-Inspired Computing Machines: Toward Novel Computational Machines*, chapter 4, pages 59–98. Presses Polytechniques et Universitaires Romandes, Lausanne, Switzerland, 1998.

110. M. Tomassini. Parallel and distributed evolutionary algorithms: A review. In K. Miettinen, M. Mäkelä, P. Neittaanmäki, and J. Periaux, editors, *Evolutionary Algorithms in Engineering and Computer Science*, pages 113–133. J. Wiley and Sons, Chichester, 1999.

111. E. C. C. Tsang, X. S. Wang, and D.S. Yeung. Improving learning accuracy of fuzzy decision trees by hybrid neural networks. *IEEE-Transactions on Fuzzy Systems*, 8(5):601–614, October 2000.

112. J. Valente de Oliveira. Semantic constraint for membership function optimization. *IEEE Transactions on Systems, Man, and Cybernetics. Part A: Systems and Humans*, 29(1):128–138, January 1999.

113. M. D. Vose. *The Simple Genetic Algorithm*. MIT Press, Cambridge, MA, August 1999.

114. P. Vuorimaa. Fuzzy self-organizing map. *Fuzzy Sets and Systems*, 66:223–231, 1994.

115. D. Whitley, S. Rana, and R. Heckendorn. Exploiting separability in search: The island model genetic algorithm. *Journal of Computing and Information Technology*, 7(1):33–47, 1999. (Special Issue on Evolutionary Computing).

116. I. H. Witten and E. Frank. *Data Mining: Practical Machine Learning Tools and Techniques with Java Implementations*. Data Management Systems. Morgan Kaufmann, San Francisco, USA, 2000.

117. A. Włoszek and P. D. Domański. Application of the coevolutionary system to the rule generation in fuzzy systems. In *Proceedings of IKAE96*, pages 203–210, Murzasichle, Poland, 1996.

118. A. Włoszek and P. D. Domański. Application of the coevolutionary system to the fuzzy model design. In *Proceedings of the Sixth IEEE International Conference on Fuzzy Systems*, volume 1, pages 391–395, 1997.

119. T.-P. Wu and S.-M. Chen. A new method for constructing membership functions and fuzzy rules from training examples. *IEEE Transactions on Systems, Man and Cybernetics, Part B: Cybernetics*, 29(1):25–40, February 1999.

120. R. R. Yager and D. P. Filev. *Essentials of Fuzzy Modeling and Control*. John Wiley & Sons., New York, 1994.

121. R. R. Yager and L. A. Zadeh. *Fuzzy Sets, Neural Networks, and Soft Computing*. Van Nostrand Reinhold, New York, 1994.

122. L. A. Zadeh. Fuzzy sets. *Information and Control*, 8:338–353, 1965.

123. L. A. Zadeh. Outline of a new approach to the analysis of complex systems and decision processes. *IEEE Transactions on Systems, Man and Cybernetics*, SMC-3(1):28–44, January 1973.

124. L. A. Zadeh. The concept of a linguistic variable and its applications to approximate reasoning. *Information Science*, Part I, 8:199-249; Part II, 8:301-357; Part III, 9:43-80., 1975.

125. S. Zahan. A fuzzy approach to computer-assisted myocardial ischemia diagnosis. *Artificial Intelligence in Medicine*, 21(1–3):271–275, January–March 2001.

Lecture Notes in Computer Science

For information about Vols. 1–3176

please contact your bookseller or Springer

Vol. 3223: K. Slind, A. Bunker, G. Gopalakrishnan (Eds.), Theorem Proving in Higher Order Logics. VIII, 337 pages. 2004.

Vol. 3222: H. Jin, G.R. Gao, Z. Xu, H. Chen (Eds.), Network and Parallel Computing. XX, 694 pages. 2004.

Vol. 3221: S. Albers, T. Radzik (Eds.), Algorithms – ESA 2004. XVIII, 836 pages. 2004.

Vol. 3220: J.C. Lester, R.M. Vicari, F. Paraguaçu (Eds.), Intelligent Tutoring Systems. XXI, 920 pages. 2004.

Vol. 3219: M. Heisel, P. Liggesmeyer, S. Wittmann (Eds.), Computer Safety, Reliability, and Security. XI, 339 pages. 2004.

Vol. 3217: C. Barillot, D.R. Haynor, P. Hellier (Eds.), Medical Image Computing and Computer-Assisted Intervention – MICCAI 2004. XXXVIII, 1114 pages. 2004.

Vol. 3216: C. Barillot, D.R. Haynor, P. Hellier (Eds.), Medical Image Computing and Computer-Assisted Intervention – MICCAI 2004. XXXVIII, 930 pages. 2004.

Vol. 3215: M.G.. Negoita, R.J. Howlett, L.C. Jain (Eds.), Knowledge-Based Intelligent Information and Engineering Systems. LVII, 906 pages. 2004. (Subseries LNAI).

Vol. 3214: M.G.. Negoita, R.J. Howlett, L.C. Jain (Eds.), Knowledge-Based Intelligent Information and Engineering Systems. LVIII, 1302 pages. 2004. (Subseries LNAI).

Vol. 3213: M.G.. Negoita, R.J. Howlett, L.C. Jain (Eds.), Knowledge-Based Intelligent Information and Engineering Systems. LVIII, 1280 pages. 2004. (Subseries LNAI).

Vol. 3212: A. Campilho, M. Kamel (Eds.), Image Analysis and Recognition. XXIX, 862 pages. 2004.

Vol. 3211: A. Campilho, M. Kamel (Eds.), Image Analysis and Recognition. XXIX, 880 pages. 2004.

Vol. 3210: J. Marcinkowski, A. Tarlecki (Eds.), Computer Science Logic. XI, 520 pages. 2004.

Vol. 3209: B. Berendt, A. Hotho, D. Mladenic, M. van Someren, M. Spiliopoulou, G. Stumme (Eds.), Web Mining: From Web to Semantic Web. IX, 201 pages. 2004. (Subseries LNAI).

Vol. 3208: H.J. Ohlbach, S. Schaffert (Eds.), Principles and Practice of Semantic Web Reasoning. VII, 165 pages. 2004.

Vol. 3207: L.T. Yang, M. Guo, G.R. Gao, N.K. Jha (Eds.), Embedded and Ubiquitous Computing. XX, 1116 pages. 2004.

Vol. 3206: P. Sojka, I. Kopecek, K. Pala (Eds.), Text, Speech and Dialogue. XIII, 667 pages. 2004. (Subseries LNAI).

Vol. 3205: N. Davies, E. Mynatt, I. Siio (Eds.), UbiComp 2004: Ubiquitous Computing. XVI, 452 pages. 2004.

Vol. 3204: C.A. Peña Reyes, Coevolutionary Fuzzy Modeling. XIII, 129 pages. 2004.

Vol. 3203: J. Becker, M. Platzner, S. Vernalde (Eds.), Field Programmable Logic and Application. XXX, 1198 pages. 2004.

Vol. 3202: J.-F. Boulicaut, F. Esposito, F. Giannotti, D. Pedreschi (Eds.), Knowledge Discovery in Databases: PKDD 2004. XIX, 560 pages. 2004. (Subseries LNAI).

Vol. 3201: J.-F. Boulicaut, F. Esposito, F. Giannotti, D. Pedreschi (Eds.), Machine Learning: ECML 2004. XVIII, 580 pages. 2004. (Subseries LNAI).

Vol. 3199: H. Schepers (Ed.), Software and Compilers for Embedded Systems. X, 259 pages. 2004.

Vol. 3198: G.-J. de Vreede, L.A. Guerrero, G. Marín Raventós (Eds.), Groupware: Design, Implementation and Use. XI, 378 pages. 2004.

Vol. 3196: C. Stary, C. Stephanidis (Eds.), User-Centered Interaction Paradigms for Universal Access in the Information Society. XII, 488 pages. 2004.

Vol. 3195: C.G. Puntonet, A. Prieto (Eds.), Independent Component Analysis and Blind Signal Separation. XXIII, 1266 pages. 2004.

Vol. 3194: R. Camacho, R. King, A. Srinivasan (Eds.), Inductive Logic Programming. XI, 361 pages. 2004. (Subseries LNAI).

Vol. 3193: P. Samarati, P. Ryan, D. Gollmann, R. Molva (Eds.), Computer Security – ESORICS 2004. X, 457 pages. 2004.

Vol. 3192: C. Bussler, D. Fensel (Eds.), Artificial Intelligence: Methodology, Systems, and Applications. XIII, 522 pages. 2004. (Subseries LNAI).

Vol. 3191: M. Klusch, S. Ossowski, V. Kashyap, R. Unland (Eds.), Cooperative Information Agents VIII. XI, 303 pages. 2004. (Subseries LNAI).

Vol. 3190: Y. Luo (Ed.), Cooperative Design, Visualization, and Engineering. IX, 248 pages. 2004.

Vol. 3189: P.-C. Yew, J. Xue (Eds.), Advances in Computer Systems Architecture. XVII, 598 pages. 2004.

Vol. 3188: F.S. de Boer, M.M. Bonsangue, S. Graf, W.-P. de Roever (Eds.), Formal Methods for Components and Objects. VIII, 373 pages. 2004.

Vol. 3187: G. Lindemann, J. Denzinger, I.J. Timm, R. Unland (Eds.), Multiagent System Technologies. XIII, 341 pages. 2004. (Subseries LNAI).

Vol. 3186: Z. Bellahsène, T. Milo, M. Rys, D. Suciu, R. Unland (Eds.), Database and XML Technologies. X, 235 pages. 2004.

Vol. 3185: M. Bernardo, F. Corradini (Eds.), Formal Methods for the Design of Real-Time Systems. VII, 295 pages. 2004.

Vol. 3184: S. Katsikas, J. Lopez, G. Pernul (Eds.), Trust and Privacy in Digital Business. XI, 299 pages. 2004.

Vol. 3183: R. Traunmüller (Ed.), Electronic Government. XIX, 583 pages. 2004.

Vol. 3182: K. Bauknecht, M. Bichler, B. Pröll (Eds.), E-Commerce and Web Technologies. XI, 370 pages. 2004.

Vol. 3181: Y. Kambayashi, M. Mohania, W. Wöß (Eds.), Data Warehousing and Knowledge Discovery. XIV, 412 pages. 2004.

Vol. 3180: F. Galindo, M. Takizawa, R. Traunmüller (Eds.), Database and Expert Systems Applications. XXI, 972 pages. 2004.

Vol. 3179: F.J. Perales, B.A. Draper (Eds.), Articulated Motion and Deformable Objects. XI, 270 pages. 2004.

Vol. 3178: W. Jonker, M. Petkovic (Eds.), Secure Data Management. VIII, 219 pages. 2004.

Vol. 3177: Z.R. Yang, H. Yin, R. Everson (Eds.), Intelligent Data Engineering and Automated Learning – IDEAL 2004. XVIII, 852 pages. 2004.